Law and Literature:
Interdisciplinary Methods of Reading

LAW AND CULTURE
BIBLIOTEK FOR RET OG KULTUR

Published with support from
Ernst Andersen og Tove Dobel Andersens Fond

Edited by
Ditlev Tamm

VOL. 1
DANSK STAFFERET
fra Reformationen til Danske Lov
Af Poul Johannes Jørgensen
By Ditlev Tamm & Helle Vogt (eds.)

VOL. 2
STUDIER I DANSK PROCESHISTORIE
Tiden indtil Danske Lov 1683
By Per Andersen

VOL. 3
LAW AND LITERATURE
Interdisciplinary Methods of Reading
By Karen-Margrethe Simonsen & Ditlev Tamm (eds.)

Karen-Margrethe Simonsen & Ditlev Tamm
(eds.)

Law and Literature:
Interdisciplinary Methods of Reading

DJØF Publishing Copenhagen
2010

Law and Literature:
Interdisciplinary Methods of Reading

First Edition 2010

© 2010 DJØF Publishing Copenhagen
Jurist- og Økonomforbundets Forlag

DJØF Publishing is a company of the
Association of Danish Lawyers and Economists

Cover: Bo Helsted
Print & Binding: Scandinavian Book, Aarhus

ISBN 978-87-574-1878-1

Published with support from

Margot and Thorvald Dreyers Fond

Sold and distributed in North America by:
International Specialized Book Services (ISBS)
Portland, OR 97213, USA
www.isbs.com

Sold in all other countries by:
DJØF Publishing Copenhagen
Denmark
www.djoef-forlag.dk

DJØF Publishing
17, Lyngbyvej
P.O.Box 2702
DK-2100 Copenhagen
Denmark

Phone: +45 39 13 55 00
Fax: +45 39 13 55 55
E-mail: forlag@djoef.dk
www.djoef-forlag.dk

Table of Contents

Introduction

Karen-Margrethe Simonsen and Ditlev Tamm

This book is based on a seminar that took place at the Carlsberg Academy in Copenhagen in March 2007. It was arranged by The Faculty of Law, Copenhagen University, represented by Professor Ditlev Tamm, and The Department of Aesthetic Studies, Aarhus University, represented by Associate Professor Karen-Margrethe Simonsen. All the contributors to this book were present and they are all pioneers within the law and literature movement, whether in the USA, Europe or the Nordic Countries.

Law and literature in the Nordic countries is a relatively new discipline especially seen from a lawyer's point of view. In Nordic humanities law and literature has been introduced as a field of study but Nordic lawyers till now with a few exceptions have not in the same way as is seen in the United States taken up this challenging subject. This small publication is therefore also meant as an introduction to law and literature as a field of interest for both lawyers and students and scholars of literature.

Law and literature has a history of uneasy relations. However, this history is a recent history. Sometimes the two disciplines have had inspiring, affirmative and complementary exchanges, at other times they have been indifferent to each other or even dismissive and excluding. Two main approaches have been characteristic for the classical studies of law and literature: You will either be looking for *law in literature* and thus take literature in which legal themes are part as your basic study. Or you may look at *law as literature* when your basic interest is the question of how legal texts may be better understood or understood differently using methods known from the study of literature. However, since the 1970's in the USA and since the 1990's in Europe, the relationship has grown stronger and become more nuanced. At the same time, the interdisciplinary field has broadened, so that it is fair today not only to talk about law and literature but also – when more disciplines than just literary studies are included – of law and humanities. The law and humanities approach, however, should not disregard the basic interest in working with literary texts and the specific conclusions that can be drawn from such a work. In the present volume the first articles can be considered relatively classical law and literature essays whereas the two final papers may be seen in the broader context of law and humanities.

The expansion, both in volume, methodology and topological comprehensiveness within the field of law and literature, has happened due to a number of social and cultural causes and also under the influence of international developments. The interest and the effort of some eminent scholars within the field have definitely had an impact on the prestige of law and literature as a subject. Today many important US Universities offer courses of law and literature whereas such courses are still not common in the curriculum of a European law school, and only occasionally occur in the curriculum at Faculties of Arts or Humanities. In Europe and in the Nordic countries institutional anchoring of law and literature is still ahead of us. But the interest for the topics and texts of law and literature is continually growing both in departments of law and literature.

Historically speaking, law and literature is a research field that has been developed mainly by lawyers in United States. That it developed here was probably no accident but has to do with the overall importance of law in American society on all levels. Another reason for the development of interest in law and literature may have been what is seen as either dilemmas inherent in the law or perhaps a growing concern for Justice awaken by signs of a crisis in law, fostered partly by a number of overt public miscarriages of law, partly by an awareness of a continuous incongruity between the norms and rights of different social groups in this multicultural society. Characteristic for many literary works that take up legal themes is therefore often some case of injustice in court or society which in a literary text can be seen as a more pure case than in reality. Also the professional lawyer as a type has been especially developed in the US. However such figures are also often found in European literature. In Europe, despite the fact that it might not be possible to talk about a serious crisis of law, the interest in law and literature can be seen as driven by similar factors. Also in Europe there is a growing awareness of the importance of law and legal institutions. This perhaps may be related to the increasing competition between national legal systems and international regulations, primarily but definitely not exclusively, regulations made by the EU and the growing importance of human rights. The international level questions national legal sovereignty, and sometimes also norms and principles of law. Law and literature is perhaps not a direct answer to this situation; but it is part of a larger questioning of or investigation into law's cultural or ethical foundations. You may also point to a general decline in the basic humanistic values and what was till recently considered general knowledge, which has led to a call for some legal subjects that try to see the law in a broader context and combine learning law with the study of some of those authors whose works are considered classic.

Though law and literature studies were invented by lawyers, many literary scholars have also shown interest in the field, mainly because it seemed like a natural continuation of tendencies already present within the field. Literary studies have traditionally been interdisciplinary and comparative, and they have always had a contextual or historical approach. There have also for a long time been studies of the law in key works by important writers like Shakespeare or Sophocles. Seen from literary studies, there is nothing radical new in law and literature. However, the interest in law and literature should be seen in coextension with new historicism and cultural studies and recently, the renewed interest in ethics and the relationship between aesthetics and politics. Law and literature force literary scholars to leave the *terrain vague* of aesthetics and see literature as part of a larger cultural context.

On the other hand, for many lawyers law and literature is a subject not only of professional duty but also of pleasure because it enables lawyers to combine reading of literature with an in-depth discussion of questions of law and morals and human ways of taking a stand that are very useful for the education of lawyers. Law and literature or law and humanities is a field that opens up for discussions based on other types of texts than those normally known from social or legal studies.

The American college and law school system has been beneficial to the education of scholars with academic knowledge within both fields, both literature and law. In Europe, scholars with a double degree are still a rare exception. This can be seen as a problem for the interdisciplinary exchange. For those who are only educated in literature there is a danger of literary abstraction. For those who are only educated in law there is a danger of reducing the interpretational complexity of aesthetic discourse.

Generally speaking, interdisciplinary research is often among the most rewarding but also among the most troublesome. Even though we all share an ideal of openness and tolerance, we are also driven by our own and homely academic interests and understanding. We might be genuinely interested in understanding how another discipline works and sees the world but in our own work, the incorporation of extra-disciplinary perspectives will more often than not be instructed by their usefulness for our own discipline. Also the understanding of the premises of the other discipline might be limited. This means that there will always be an irreducible asymmetry in the interaction between the two disciplines. What literature wants from law, might be something completely different from what law itself sees as ruling or cutting-edge principles. Likewise, law may understand literature and literary interpretation in a completely different way than literary scholars.

Interdisciplinary research is risky business, but – as already said – most rewarding if it is a success. It opens the horizon of the home discipline, puts basic question in a new way and even makes you question home-grown norms and vocabulary. One of the important tasks of law and literature or law and humanities is to increase mutual awareness and knowledge of theory and methodology between the two disciplines. A fruitful discussion necessarily implies knowledge within both fields. But the best interdisciplinary research is in fact not research where two disciplines confront each other but where they interrelate in such a way that they create what you may see as a third critical space between them. This is possible also because – despite all their differences – lawyers and literary scholars share a very basic interest, namely an interest in rhetoric and narration and in reading and interpretation. Both lawyers (practicing lawyers and researchers) and literary academics and critics are occupied with texts of different kinds.

Both for literary and legal scholars there are some 'master texts' or a canon that are widely discussed and to which we keep recurring. Sophocles, Shakespeare, Melville, Dostojevskij, Kafka, Camus and in a broader sense, Kant, Hegel, Montesquieu, Hobbes and others are examples of authors who will be canon for both literary and legal scholars. In this book focus is on literary texts and more general, on the role of narration. What happens when literary and legal scholars respectively read and interpret the law in literary texts? And what role does narration play in the cultural understanding of law?

In this book we want to bring lawyers and literary scholars together in a common discussion of texts thus creating a very concrete dialogue between the two disciplines. Today so many approaches have been legitimized within law and literature and law and humanities that it sometimes seems difficult to determine by reading an article whether the author is a lawyer or a social scientist or a scholar from the humanities. Still there might be some basic differences that become visible in the concrete reading of literature and law. The idea of bringing lawyers and literary scholars together in this common endeavour of reading texts is to illuminate both similarities and differences, thus opening the interdisciplinary dialogue on the textual interpretation of law. In order to do so, it is important that the authors of the articles come from both law and literature.

In the book we have essays by three literary scholars and two legal scholars and one opening essay by Professor Richard Weisberg who has a double degree of law and literature. We hope that this dual perspective of reading both contribute to a new understanding of the texts in question and to a more nuanced understanding of similarities and differences between legal and literary readings.

Contributors and contributions

Richard Weisberg is Walter Floersheimer Professor of Constitutional Law at Benjamin N. Cardozo Law School New York, and a Director for the Center for Holocaust Studies, New York. He is a specialist in constitutional law and law and literature. Selected publications: *The Failure of the Word* (1984), *Poethics and Other Strategies of Law and literature* (1992) and *Vichy Law and the Holocaust in France*, 1996. He has a double degree in law and literature and is a pioneer in the American law and literature movement. Since the 1970's he has contributed substantially to the creation of the research field of law and literature, and some of his books are now master-texts within law and literature, for instance *Failure of the* Word (1984) and *Poethics and Other Strategies of Law and Literature* (1992). In his contribution to this book, he presents an 'exegetic' reading of justices and injustices in Katherine Anne Porter's story 'Noon Wine'. He is especially interested in, how this story from 1937 presents the lawyer and raises the question whether following the law means providing justice.

Justice is also an important concern in the article by Jeanne Gaakeer. Gaakeer is both a Judge in the criminal law section at the Appellate Court in The Hague and Professor of Legal Theory at Erasmus University of Rotterdam. She is a specialist in philosophy of law and the interdisciplinary relations between medicine, law and literature. She has written various books and articles on law and literature, for instance the book: *Hope Springs Eternal. An Introduction to the Work of James Boyd White* (1998). Together with Francois Ost she has edited *Crossing Borders: Law, Language and Literature* (2008). In her article, she makes a close reading of William Shakespeare's *Othello*, where she draws the attention to the 'hazards of legal interpretation' and shows how literature can have significance for lawyers, especially when the case is against defendants suffering from mental impediments.

In the next article we stay with Shakespeare but now seen from the viewpoint of a literary scholar. Leif Dahlberg is a doctor of comparative literature and Associate Professor, Royal Institute of Technology, Stockholm. He is a specialist in legal spaces and re-readings of literary classics by Shakespeare, Kafka and others. Among other publications, he has written 'Emotional tropes in the courtroom. On representation of affect and emotion in legal court proceedings', *Nordic Theatre Studies* 21 (2009) and 'Achilles' foot and the Law: Legal Space(s), Striated and Smooth', in *Practicing Equity, Addressing Law: Equity in Law and Literature*, (2008). He reads *The Merchant of Venice* with a special emphasis not only on the presentation of law in the play but also on the performance of law. In contrast with recent readings of the play that stress the tragic aspects of the play, for instance the punishment and exclusion of the Jew Shylock, Dahlberg argues controversially that the play conforms with the rules of the genre of comedy, which also entails a strengthening of community and social inclusion. Dahlberg bases his reading on aesthetic genre-conventions that in this example operate against modern ethical assumptions.

Arild Linneberg is a Professor at the Department of Comparative Literature, University of Bergen, Norway. He is a specialist in semiotics, literary criticism, law in literature, and he has published numerous books and articles on law and literature for instance in *Tretten triste essays om krig og litteratur* (2001) and in *12 ½ tale om litteratur og lov og rett* (2007). In his article on Camus, he stresses how the two parts of *L'étranger* show two different types of language-constructed reality which deconstruct each other and thus question the foundation of legal discourse. He also discusses the relationship between the judgment of Meursault, author of the murder of one Arab and the French regime who killed thousands of Arabs for political reasons. Thus the main aim of the article is to show law's dependency on language and history.

The last two articles take up the discussion of narration's importance for the understanding of human rights; or to put it differently: the importance of narrations of human rights for cultural identity.

The first of these articles is written by Helle Porsdam, who is a professor of History at Saxo Institute, Copenhagen University. She is a specialist in American Studies and cultural studies more specifically the role and function of law in American society, human rights, and copyright. Her doctoral thesis is the book *Legally Speaking: contemporary American culture and the law* (1999), and her latest book is *From Civil to Human Rights. Dialogues on Law and Humanities in the United States and Europe* (2009) In her article, she argues that 'human rights talk' may be that cultural glue that we need in a Europe, still traumatized by second world war experiences and ridden by national and ethnic differences. Human Rights are not only rights specified in the vocabulary of law, they may constitute the basis of general cultural narratives. She gives three examples of interrelated narratives that have to do with human rights: female rights, consumption rights, and copyright.

The second of the articles on human rights is written by Sten Schaumburg-Müller who is a Professor of law and legal jurisprudence at the Department of Law, Aarhus University and a specialist in human rights in an historical, philosophical and cultural context. His doctoral thesis has come out as a book, *Fem retsfilosofiske teser* (2009) and he has written on human rights in many different contexts, for instance in 'Fire fordomme om menneskerettigheder – og et kritisk juridisk blik' in *Semikolon*, 7, no. 14 (2007). In his introductory remarks, Schaumburg-Müller notes a certain imbalance in law and literature studies in Denmark in favour of literature or humanistic studies in general. He therefore argues in favour of establishing an equal footing and ventures into the discussion not only about narratives about law but law in itself as a narrative of identity. Saying what we accept and what we do not is to create a cultural identity. However, in a Danish (and maybe European) context, human rights-talk is in opposition to a historically strong tradition of political consensus and *volonté general*.

The editors wish to thank Professor Helle Porsdam for her encouragement and support of the project. We also wish to thank Dreyers Foundation (Dreyers Fond) for their financial support.

The editors

Ditlev Tamm: Professor of legal history at the Faculty of Law, Copenhagen University. He is a specialist on legal history, comparative law and roman law. He has also published books in the field of political history, literature and ballet and general cultural studies.

Karen-Margrethe Simonsen: Associate Professor at Section for Comparative Literature, Dep. of Aesthetic Studies, Aarhus University. She is a specialist in literary history, world literature and law in literature, for instance in works by Sophocles, Kleist and Musil and has authored several publications in this field.

Rich, Sweet, and Tender
vs. Sour, Displeased and Upset:

Two Ways of Seeing Things in 'Noon Wine'

Richard H. Weisberg

Insufficiently known, even among Law and Literature devotees, Katherine Anne Porter's wonderful story 'Noon Wine' should be part of the canon. Together with Susan Glaspell's terrific 'A Jury of her Peers',[1] this story offers a particular early 20th century American female voice: In their subtle narratives, Porter and Glaspell ultimately encourage more than their reader's skepticism about male-centered legal institutions and reasoning. They express, each in her own way, a kind of revulsion for the male legal figure, one that rivals the Dickensian nausea before the far more elaborated portraits of Tulkinghorn, Vholes, and Guppy.[2]

I want briefly to introduce the reader to Porter's story, or to embellish my already conversant readers' appreciation of it. My aim is to answer the question 'How (as opposed to what) does the story mean'?[3] My method is the classical explication de texte. The latter permits me to take two passages, look at them reasonably closely, and draw some conclusions as to the way meaning arises in 'Noon Wine'. It also permits – nay requires – that I recount along the way the broad outlines of the tale's 'action'.

On a dusty and run-down dairy farm in the American southwest at the turn of the 19th Century, the Thompson family lives and works. Mr. Thompson is 'a tough weather-beaten man' who has let the farm deteriorate more from disinterest than venality. His wife, in Mr. Thompson's words 'ain't very strong'. They have two growing, healthy sons, a bit undisciplined and not yet ready to

---

1. Originally published as a play, 'Trifles' in 1916 and then published in an expanded form as a short story a few years later in Ellery Queen's *Mystery Magazine*.
2. See my *Poethics and other Strategies of Law and Literature*.
3. The titular phrase in John Ciardi, 'How does a Poem Mean' (1959).

take over from their Dad the task of improving the family's economic situation.

Into this environment, where ends barely meet, a stranger arrives. Mr. Helton, an exceptionally quiet Swede who has come down apparently from North Dakota, asks for work. His rate is low enough that Thompson gives him a job and his own modest quarters in a shack near the main house. Mrs. Thompson, trying to survive one of her many days of illness, has not been consulted, and her first reaction at having to house and feed the new worker is one of anger:

> Heavens, he [Helton] looked lazy and worthless, he did, now ... It was just like Mr. Thompson to take on that kind. She did wish he would be more considerate, and take a little trouble with his business. She wanted to believe in her husband, and there were too many times when she couldn't. She wanted to believe that tomorrow, or at least the day after, life, such a battle at best, was going to be better. (Porter)

Porter conveys the turnaround in her attitude in one fabulous paragraph early in the story, which I will divide in half to give my reader pause:

> Rickety wooden shelves clung at hazard in the square around the small pool where the larger pails of milk and butter stood, fresh and sweet in the cold water. One hand supporting her flat, pained side, the other shading her eyes, Mrs. Thompson leaned over and peered into the pails. The cream had been skimmed and set aside, there was a rich roll of butter, the wooden molds and shallow pans had been scrubbed and scalded for the first time in who knows when, the barrel was full of buttermilk ready for the pigs and the weanling calves, the hard-packed dirt floor had been swept smooth. Mrs. Thompson straightened up again, smiling tenderly. She had been ready to scold him, a poor man who needed a job, who had just come there and who might not have been expected to do things properly at first. There was nothing she could do to make up for the injustice she had done him in her thoughts but to tell him how she appreciated his good clean work, finished already, in no time at all. ... (Porter)

The passage to this point conveys a turn from anger to pleasure, from unfair appraisal to just appreciation, from physical illness to spiritual strength, and from bitterness to sweetness. And all of this is done by connecting the reader to her weak eyes' visual path as she observes with increasing joy the 'fresh and sweet' milk, the 'rich rolls of butter,' the skimmed cream and the full barrel of buttermilk. The decay of the farm's recent past, which matches in the early descriptions her own body's unhealthiness, has been quickly transformed by this stranger into a festival of richness, if not yet economic, then certainly sensual. And it has all been done with a cleanliness you can almost touch through the mediation of Mrs. Thompson's eyes.

It is not for nothing, as we shall see, that the passage squeezes out the 'injustice' she had done to Mr. Helton in her thoughts, as it also dispatches the poverty, the sloppiness, and the thin-ness of the farm's productivity prior to this *coup de foudre*. And we shall see, also, that the effusiveness of her self-correction towards Helton will soon benefit – if only for a time – Mr. Thompson himself. But first, the paragraph winds down and permits the transformed woman to pronounce her new judgment of – and to – the taciturn Swede:

> She ventured near the door of the shack with her careful steps; Mr. Helton opened his eyes, stopped playing [his harmonica], and brought his chair down straight, but did not look at her, or get up. She was a little frail woman with long thick brown hair in a braid, a suffering patient mouth and diseased eyes which cried easily. She wove her fingers into an eyeshade, thumbs on temples, and, winking her tearful lids, said with a polite little manner, 'Howdy do, sir. I'm Miz Thompson, and I wanted to tell you you did real well in the milk house. It's always been a hard place to keep. (Porter)

Helton's peripheral vision confirms our impression of Mrs. Thompson as a sickly lady. But she can hope he will take her words of strength and of justice literally, even or especially as emerging from such a weak vessel as herself. If the laconic newly hired hand does not or cannot do so, Mrs. Thompson will manage to transfer from him to her husband – and in short order, too – the warmth of her new feelings; it is after dinner the same day, and the married couple are alone:

> He gave her a good pinch on her thin little rump. 'No more meat on you than a rabbit,' he said, fondly. 'Now I like 'em cornfed.'
>
> Mrs. Thompson looked at him open-eyed and blushed. She could see better by lamplight. 'Why Mr. Thompson, sometimes I think you're the evilest-minded man that ever lived.' She took a handful of hair on the crown of his head and gave it a good, slow pull. 'That's to show you how it feels, pinching so hard when you're supposed to be playing,' she said, gently. (Porter)

And so the transformative day ends, with the many adverbs first associated with the milk-house scene and Helton ('tenderly', 'properly', 'easily') now transmuted to the domestic kitchen – and who knows if not a bit later to the conjugal bed ('fondly', 'gently'). Things are looking up – fairness and love are being doled out at the Thompson farm – temporarily. For, although it may take a few years of relative prosperity and relative family happiness – all brought about by the arrival of Mr. Helton – *law* eventually rears its ungentle, untender, uneasy head.

In fact, there is only one portent of doom as the prosperous years roll along. Continuing to benefit from the Swede's productivity and self-effacing efficiency, the four Thompson's have even adjusted to his peculiarity: playing the same song over and over again on his collection of harmonicas. They adjust to the repetitiveness, learning only later of a history connected to the song's title, which is 'Noon Wine'. But one incident foreshadows the bitter entrance of law into the sweet, rich environment of the post-Helton dairy farm. Mrs. Thompson observes the taciturn hired hand violently shaking her two boys after the lads poked around among his harmonicas and even started to play a few of them. Shocked by this sole display of physical violence, she confronts her sons, and after telling Mr. Thompson about it, the incident is resolved within the confines of the family. The boys are mildly chastised by their parents, and life proceeds as before.

But Helton's violence is part of his own past that the song he plays also evokes. It is left to an interloper, years after the Swede's successful work has transformed the Thompson homestead from rickety famine to squeaky clean abundance, to uncover the wild history of this laconic man. A certain Homer T. Hatch barges in on the quiet of Mr. Thompson's plenitude to inform him that Helton is wanted for murder back up in North Dakota. Incredulous, Thompson tries to dissuade Hatch from grabbing the fugitive and claiming the bounty he will receive from the northern authorities. But Hatch, a distasteful individual in his manner as well as his mission, will not be put off. "The law,' said Mr. Hatch, 'is solidly behind me." And the song Helton plays, he tells Thompson, is a remnant of the hidden madness that brought about the murder: 'One of the Scandahoovians told me what it meant. ... Especially that part about getting so gay you jus' go ahead and drink up all the likker you got on hand before noon. It seems like up in them Swede countries a man carries a bottle of wine around with him as a matter of course ...'

The end of the Helton years threatened by this 'no good' bounty hunter and his tale of a quiet man's insane past is too much for Thompson to accept, and he grabs his ax. Confused by the heat and the discombulating news, he seems to hallucinate a knifeblade being thrust by Hatch into the suddenly encroaching body of Helton himself. Thompson brings down the ax 'on Mr. Hatch's head as if he were stunning a beef.'

Mrs. Thompson arrives on the bloody scene in time to see that there has been no attack on Helton, no knife-blade, just an act of homicidal violence by her husband that will change their lives forever. Helton will be incarcerated and returned to the authorities up north. As for Mr. Thompson, he needs a good criminal lawyer. He finds one in Mr. Burleigh, the best the bar offers in their locality, and one who will show the reader 'how it means' to be a lawyer.

Distraught at the disconnection between his own wild imaginings of how the homicide occurred and the accurate observations of his wife – she has been established as the tale's oracular (if sickly) presence – Mr. Thompson receives excellent advice from counsel. The community, Mr. Burleigh is certain, will not convict a man for killing someone 'coming to your house on such an errand. Why hell, said Mr. Burleigh, that wasn't even manslaughter you committed. So now you just hold your horses and keep your shirt on. And don't say one word without I tell you.'

The lawyer proves to be correct. Mr. Thompson is acquitted. Once paid his 'reasonable fee,' however, the busy practitioner wants nothing more from his former client. And Thompson's feverish refusal to find 'closure' even in the verdict of his peers drives the overwrought farmer back into Burleigh's office, as though still seeking assurances beyond those of the justice system.

It is precisely here, at the end of the mere three paragraphs devoted to Burleigh and the trial that we are made to see and feel the difference in the face of success that divides the sweetness and justice of Mrs. Thompson from the hard pragmatics of the law:

> ... [A]fter it was over, Mr. Burleigh didn't seem pleased to see him when he got to dropping in the office to talk it over, telling him things that had slipped his mind at first; trying to explain what an ornery low hound Mr. Hatch had been, anyhow. Mr. Burleigh seemed to have lost interest; he looked sour and upset when he saw Mr. Thompson at the door. (Porter)

The adverb 'sour' speaks volumes and cements this little scene into the reader's increasing awareness of the brilliance of this tale. We cannot help but be reminded of that earlier narrative locus of adjectives, abstract nouns, and adverbs, all evoking the delighted turnabout in Mrs. Thompson's judgment of her new hired hand. In the lawyer's office, 'tenderly' and 'gently' have been brutally replaced by 'sour' and 'upset', and all the richness of the

Richard H. Weisberg

butter and the cleanliness of the shed have been superceded by nastiness, nastiness that is as much a part of the work of a successful lawyer as correcting
an 'injustice' done to a fine new hired hand is part of being a successful
farmer.

Narrative fiction of the 19th and 20th century contains many acerbic portraits of lawyers. Mr. Burleigh in his understated and under-narrated way belongs in the rogues gallery of men who do their legal work well, but fail hor-
ribly in the domain of the human, even or especially where – as here – it
overlaps with their legal responsibilities. Something happens to the man of
the law along the path to professional success. Had Mr. Burleigh retained a
bit of Mrs. Thompson's sweet sense of justice, he would have seen that the
acquittal he had procured needed further elaboration or else his client would
go off the deep end ... His sourness and injustice help bring the tale to its
eventual end.

Bibliography

Porter, Katherine Anne. 'Noon Wine'. In *The Collected Stories of Katherine Anne Porter*.
    Harcourt Brace 1972 (1937): 222-68.
Weisberg, Richard H. *Poethics and other Strategies of Law and Literature*. New York:
    Columbia University Press 1992.

'The Bloody Book of Law'

Some Remarks on the Interrelation of Law, Medicine, and the Behavioral Sciences in William Shakespeare's
The Tragedy of Othello, the Moor of Venice'

Jeanne Gaakeer

1. Introduction

When the Duke of Venice pledges his word of honor to Brabanzio that he is to choose a fitting punishment for the man who stole his daughter, he says, 'the bloody book of law you shall yourself read in the bitter letter after your own sense' (I.3.67-69).[1] At the end of the play, with hindsight, we understand that this commitment was also a prediction that did not augur well for any of the protagonists. By then we have seen Othello read, or rather misread, the human condition.

I have chosen this line in order to suggest for purposes of this book a reading of the Othello case, or rather, two, because the more I read, the more perspectives I perceived that are important for lawyers. Both readings aim to draw the attention to the hazards of legal interpretation, not in the sense of the interpretation of the texts of law, but the interpretation of evidence and a defendant's personal circumstances. I would like to suggest to you, first, the play's significance for lawyers when it comes to judging defendants suffering from mental impediments, and second, the play's lessons for our professional attitude as lawyers, and more specifically, judges. The key to both readings is Othello's epilepsy.

---

1. The edition used for purposes of citation in this paper is: Stephen Greenblatt, and others eds. *The Norton Shakespeare*, based on the Oxford edition by S. Wells and G. Taylor eds. New York and London: W.W. Norton and Co., 1997.

2. The Othello case

I would like you to consider, if only for this moment, a different ending of the play. What would have happened, if Othello had not committed suicide? Suppose you were the defense lawyer in the Othello case. What could you possibly say to defend your client who is so obviously the victim of Iago's resentment? Here's what I think I would do, in the European legal tradition.

Your Honors, may it please the court,

My client, Othello the Moor, has lived his life in the service of the country, and his is an impeccable record. Yet today he stands here before you to give account for his having slain his wife. As far as the evidence is concerned, I shall be brief, for it is conclusive. My client pleads guilty to the act which might be defined as first-degree, premeditated murder. With regard to the life sentence the prosecutor wants you to impose, however, I beg to differ. Of course you will judge my client by his actions and find him guilty as far as these are concerned. But before passing sentence you must decide whether my client is fully liable for what he did. Only then can you decide on the penalty. My client wants all circumstances of the case discussed here before you. He told me, 'Speak of me as I am. Nothing extenuate' (V.2.351). That is exactly what I am going to do, because the fact that my client thinks of himself as, '... one not easily jealous, but, being wrought, perplex'd in the extreme' (V.2.354-355) shows us his epistemological insight in the causality of events, even if it comes too late.

Primarily, I would like you to consider the possibility that Othello committed the murder under duress, because his ensign Iago is the external force under the pressure of which Othello has acted, and this pressure was such that he could not reasonably resist it. That is why he must be excused, because his will as an element of criminal intent – though present at the time of the murder – was impaired to such a degree that he cannot be blamed for the act he committed. Thus a constituent element in the criminal charge is missing, and that is why discharge is your only option. Should you find no legal basis for this decision, I would alternatively suggest to you that we have here a case of diminished responsibility. The act cannot fully be attributed to my client. The reports of the forensic psychiatrist, dr. Robert Burton, whose theory of the humours I am sure you are familiar with, show the influence of Othello's epilepsy on his actions. And they show that this influence is to such an extent that his mental state, or should we say dis-

ease, at the time of the crime was such, that we have here a case of diminished responsibility. Therefore, I would like you to consider, in a
just and fair manner, the option of imposing a more lenient penalty, or,
if necessary impose an entrustment order so that my client can be
treated for his mental problems.

This plea, hypothetical though it is, is Othello's only option. For a favorable
outcome, it is absolutely necessary to define Othello's pathological jealousy
as the effect of his neurological syndrome on his actions. No doubt, Othello,
as we know him from the play, will not like this defense strategy at all, because the unintended side effect of his case is that he goes down in history as
the name giver of the syndrome, mostly affecting males, which is characterized by morbid pathological jealousy resulting in accusations and tests of the
spouse's infidelity. It is a neurological disorder, closely connected, and I
think not incidentally, to epilepsy, among others.[2] This delusional disorder –
characterized by the presence of non-bizarre delusions, i.e. that the situation
can occur in real life such as being deceived by one's spouse – can lead to
acts of violence such as homicide and suicide.[3] And there is more to it, to
which I will return shortly, viz. that cognitive psychology, and experimental
psychology suggest that persons with delusions selectively attend to available
information, and are prone to draw conclusions on the basis of insufficient
information.

3. God-sent disease?

Shakespeare introduces the subject of epilepsy most subtly when he has Brabanzio reproach Othello for having won Desdemona by witchcraft, 'Damned
as thou art, thou hast enchanted her, ... thou has practised on her with foul
charms' (I.2.64 and 74). Without 'witchcraft' (I.3.64) Othello couldn't have

---

2. The Othello syndrome was named by the English psychiatrist John Todd (1914-1987),
   see J. Todd and K. Dewhurst, 'The Othello Syndrome: a study in the psychopathology
   of sexual jealousy' (367-374). Also of interest, Lance Fogan, MD, 'The Neurology in
   Shakespeare' (922-924); Christopher G. Goetz MD, 'Shakespeare in Charcot's Neurologic teaching' (920-921); Yury Furman, MD, and others, 'Shakespeare and sleep
   disorders' (1171-1172).
3. DSM-IV-TR = Diagnostic Manual of Mental Disorders, fourth edition, text revision
   2000, defines delusions as false beliefs based on incorrect inference about external reality that persist despite the evidence to the contrary.

pulled it off, so Desdemona is 'corrupted by spells and medicines bought of mountebanks' (I.3.60). The ancient Greek idea that epilepsy was a sacred disease sent by the gods – with the state of seizures thought to impart prophesying abilities to the patient – had in Renaissance Europe been transformed into the notion that epilepsy was directly connected with witchcraft and/or necromancy.

No wonder the crucial object of the play and Desdemona's ruin is the handkerchief 'spotted with strawberries' (III.3. 438-39) and with 'magic in the web' (III.4.67). An Egyptian sorceress gave it to Othello's mother and warned her to keep it to ensure her husband's love. That handkerchief is both directly and indirectly the cause of Othello's seizures. But we mustn't get ahead of our story, because first there is that other sorcerer, Iago, a 'seemer' who pretends to place his intelligence in the service of the other but bends all to his will. 'I am not what I am' (I.1.65), he says, and that is how he will be exposed because he is not whom he looks like. Iago is 'honest'[4] but that is on purpose, 'seeming so for my peculiar end' (I.1.60) and that end is Othello's fall.

Is his aim revenge because he thinks his wife Emilia had an affair with Othello? Does he harbour a grudge against Othello who chose Michael Cassio as his right-hand man? That is left open to our interpretation. More important is his other argument, 'The Moor is of a free and open nature, that thinks men honest that but seem to be so, and will as tenderly be led by th'nose as asses are' (I.3.381-384). The tragic irony is this. Iago is the innate cynic whose Claggart-like[5] aversion to goodness in others finds in Othello an easy prey for its malice.

And his opportunity to strike comes fairly soon when in the relative ease of his stay in Cyprus – the Turkish fleet was shipwrecked before Othello could engage it in battle – Othello falls prey to Iago's first trap. When Michael Cassio asks Desdemona to intercede on his behalf and promote his rehabilitation with Othello, this action is grist to Iago's mill. He starts his insinuations, suggests the impropriety of their dealings.

What 'is', i.e. Cassio's request to Desdemona to plead his case before Othello, becomes what 'seems', an adulterous relationship. Iago is cunning.

---

4. All say so, Cassio, 'Good night, honest Iago' (II.3.309), Desdemona, 'O, that's an honest fellow' (III.3.5), Othello, 'Iago is most honest' (II.3.6). For another example of Iago's 'honesty', see (II.1.197-198), 'But I'll set down the pegs that make this music, as honest as I am'.
5. The reference here is to the master-at-arms Claggart in Herman Melville's novella *Billy Budd, Sailor*.

He avoids direct attack. The poison of jealousy poured into Othello's veins does not fail, as Iago is pleased to find out, 'But I do see you're moved' (III.3.221).

Othello's emotion subsequently shows in the first of a number of strange exchanges he has with Desdemona. Asked whether he is ill, Othello speaks of pain in the forehead. Is it self-mockery, referring to the horns that grow on the cuckolded husband's head, or the onset of an epileptic attack? Desdemona thinks it's his hard work and the wakeful nights as an officer of the watch, 'Faith, that's with watching' (III.3.289), but there's the rub of the hidden meaning of 'watching', because in his mind's eye Othello 'sees' Cassio and Desdemona having sex. Iago's plan gains momentum when Desdemona tries to bind Othello's forehead with her handkerchief to ease the pain. Unfit for the purpose the handkerchief drops to the floor and is found by Emilia who has been pestered for it by Iago. The tension is heightened as Iago sees his chances multiplied, 'Have you not sometimes seen a handkerchief spotted with strawberries in your wife's hand? (III.3.438-39) ... '... such a handker-chief ... did I today see Cassio wipe his beard with' (III.3.442-444).

In the meantime Desdemona discusses Othello's state of mind with Emilia. Surely he cannot be jealous, because, 'I think the sun where he was born drew all such humours from him' (III.4.27-28). She is as literal a reader of the human mind as Othello and fails to notice that Iago manipulates them. Sadly it is Othello's literal interpretation of Iago's honesty that makes him doubt his wife's honesty and chastity. And Desdemona is mistaken, for there is definitely something wrong with Othello's humours. The Renaissance *to-pos* of the humours is interwoven with Othello's clinical picture. Othello holds it against Desdemona that her hand is, 'Hot, hot and moist' (III.4.37), a sign of a licentious way of life. He asks for her handkerchief for his eyes, for, '... a salt and sorry rheum offends' him (III.4.48-49). Desdemona fails to produce the handkerchief, of course, and she is in distress, 'My lord is not my lord, nor should I know him were he in favour as in humour altered' (III.4.120).

Cassio has by then given the handkerchief, – evidence planted in his bed-room by Iago – to Bianca. Othello mistakes a meeting of Cassio and Bianca for a love-scene between Cassio and Desdemona and this triggers an epileptic seizure. Othello, that literal reader with an empiricist bent who wants 'ocular proof' (III.3.365) of Desdemona's infidelity, lets Iago be his eyes and be-lieves what Iago offers as literal hearsay evidence. '... my medicine works' (IV.1.42), says Iago when he sees the triumph of his verbal venom. 'My lord is fall'n into an epilepsy. This is his second fit. He had one yesterday'

(IV.1.47-48). Othello's emotional agitation has exacerbated to the extreme and is discharged in a seizure.

When Cassio offers to rub Othello's temples, Iago prevents it, 'No, forbear. The lethargy must have his quiet course. If not, he foams at mouth, and by and by breaks out to savage madness' (IV.1.49-53). The latter is prospective, because it is precisely in another fit that Othello will kill Desdemona. But before that, there is yet another talk between Othello and Desdemona, showing impending danger when Othello calls Desdemona, 'that cunning whore of Venice' (IV.2.93).

Afterwards Desdemona desperately questions Emilia on the subject of jealousy. When Emilia explains, 'But jealous souls will not be answered so. They are not ever jealous for the cause, but jealous for they're jealous. It is a monster begot upon itself, born upon itself', Desdemona sighs, 'Heaven keep the monster from Othello's mind' (III.4.155-158). Iago's comforting words, 'Tis but his humour' (IV.2.169) have once more that ironic quality of being and seeming, which Shakespeare now draws to its logical conclusion. When Othello hits Desdemona, prelude to a fatal ending, Iago explains, 'he's that he is' (IV.1.267). Painfully true is Iago's remark about Cassio's 'apparent' deceit, 'Men should be what they seem, or those that be not, would they might seem none' (III.3.132-133).

Othello has had two seizures within two days and his third is fatal to Desdemona. With his persuasive and constant repetition of the charge, and his continuous machinations Iago has systematically planted the notion of Desdemona's infidelity in Othello's head, and this makes Othello literally foam at the mouth. Desdemona recognizes the evil omen,

> And yet I fear you, for you're fatal then when your eyes roll so ... Alas, why gnaw you so your nether lip? Some bloody passion shakes your very frame. These are portents, but yet I hope, I hope they do not point on me. (V.2.39-40, and V.2.46-49).

Seeming coincides with being, and Othello kills Desdemona in this third attack of what he himself calls, '... the very error of the moon, she comes more nearer earth than she was wont, and makes men mad' (V.2.118-120).

4. Othello as a mirror for magistrates

The play teaches us not to jump to 'foregone conclusions' (III.3.433), to resist closure. From the very start we would like to warn Othello, 'Don't do it', but we need the full anamnesis and subsequent catharsis in the classical senses described by Aristotle, even though we might prefer amnesia for all protagonists.

a. The Body as a Clock

As students of law we understand how Othello's 'bloody passion' fits that 'bloody book of law'. As students of medicine we recognize Othello's complex partial seizures in the blank look or empty stare, suggesting impairment of consciousness. As if straight from a twenty-first-century textbook of neurology, Shakespeare offers us the seizures, which last a couple of minutes and are followed by a state of confusion lasting longer. He paints the headaches and sudden, inexplicable changes of mood, he shows us the effect of stress-related negative emotions. Did he know that the limbic system, the portion of the brain that regulates emotion, is one of the most common places for seizures to begin?

Of course not, but our Renaissance man undoubtedly knew something else, and that is the theory of the humours introduced, in the fourth century B.C. by Hippocrates, in his *On the Nature of Man*, with melancholy as the essential humour, cause of many diseases and problems. And besides, Shakespeare had been on the cast of his friend Ben Jonson's 1598 production of *Every Man in his Humour*. So he did not have to wait for the 1621 publication of Robert Burton's *The Anatomy of Melancholy*, an account of the dichotomies of blood and phlegm, choler and melancholy that control a person's temperament.[6] If blood is the dominant humour, passionate emotion – Othellos' love for Desdemona – is the result. If choler, then anger – ' Ay, let her rot and perish, and be damned tonight' (IV.1.174), 'I will chop her into messes. Cuckold me!' (IV.1.190). The watery eyes, the 'salt and sorry rheum' (III.4.49) are they not a sign of an excess of phlegm, which leads to a moist brain affected by epilepsy? And yes, an imbalance in the humours and the human brain – 'for our body is like a clock; if one wheel be amiss, all the rest are disordered, the whole fabric suffers' – can be caused by sorcery, says Burton (Supra note 6, Member III, subsection II).

6. Burton, R., *The Anatomy of Melancholy*, at 147, First partition, section I, member II, subsection II 'Division of the Body, Humours, Spirits'. The 4 humours are: blood (hot, sweet and temperate); pituita or phlegm (cold and moist); choler (hot, dry and bitter); melancholy (cold and dry, black and sour, a bridle to the other two hot humours, blood and choler), and 'These four humours have some analogy with the four elements, and to the four ages of man'.

27

'Case in point', says the lawyer, 'that's Iago!'. 'No, it's the epilepsy, stupid!', says the neurologist. And they are both right. One of the three faculties discerned by Burton is the rational mind, and this being disturbed by the epilepsy, disturbs the will also in the sense of criminal intent.

'Tis in ourselves that we are thus or thus. Our bodies are gardens, to the which our wills are gardeners' (I.3.316-318), or so Iago claims, with his willful destruction of Othello. That this is not the case for Othello is what Shakespeare holds before us with the ambiguity of seeming and being. Iago is convinced that man can pretend to be who he wants to be. Othello's will does not have control over his body, given the classical example of the imbalance of his humours. In all his physical complexity Othello is the perfect subject for physiological, neurological, and psychological investigation; because of his actions he is prime material for the lawyer.

Taken together he is a *must* for the interdisciplinary discussion of lawyers, physicians, and behavioral scientists. How about determinism and the concepts of volition and agency?[7] What about Iago's unlawful threat and the doctrine of excuse defenses? What about the combination of objective, situational aspects such as the situation in Cyprus, and the subjective, individual factors, such as a marriage to a woman above his station, and his medical predisposition? This is grist to the mill of your average lawyer. 'How on earth can a lawyer judge about a defendant's medical and/or mental condition?', sighs the physician who is called to court to testify as an expert witness.

As far as I am concerned, and this would be my first conclusion, the Othello case can and should be read as a warning to professionals. From a *Law in Literature* perspective it is a mirror for magistrates[8] who will have to incorporate into their judgments the findings of other disciplines, medicine and psychiatry. With our western history of ideas in hindsight, we are, paradoxically perhaps, at the same time also warned against an excessive, empiricist belief in the data of the natural sciences.

b. Habits of the Mind

What I mean is this, and this would be my second reading of the play for purposes of this book, the play also forces us to reflect on our evidentiary standards, our interpretive assumptions, the nature of motivation and the grounds stated in judgments, the weight of hearsay evidence, physical and

---

7. The criminal anthropologist Lombroso's disciple Enrico Ferri describes Othello as an oversensitive man, prone to neurological 'extremes'.
8. Locus classicus is William Baldwin's *The Mirror for Magistrates* (1559).

eyewitness evidence, in short, the power of visual epistemology and empiricism.

Othello judges Desdemona's presumed intentions, not her external actions, and once he witnesses, or rather thinks he has witnessed a person's act – think of Cassio and Bianca – he assumes a guilty act, and does not look for evidence. So the only thing he wants to prove is his assumption of Desdemona's infidelity which is both an example of, in psychological and legal terms, the confirmation bias with respect to what we know is his delusion, and it is also a form of belief perseverance.

The confirmation bias is the inclination to seek and interpret evidence in such a manner that it confirms an existing conviction, expectation, or hypothesis, and in Othello's case a delusion. That is to say, we have an idea or intuition with respect to the world around us, and this becomes our guideline when we try to gather, and, after that, judge evidence. '*Da mihi facta, dabo tibi ius*', says the jurist, 'give me the facts, and I will give you (the) law'. But lawyers all too often forget David Hume's lesson that the world of facts is in fact a habit of the mind. Our mind. The, often disordering, reality of literature shows us this, and keeps us from legal myopia. Jumping to a foregone conclusion – 'though it be but a dream' (III.3.434) as Shakespeare warns us – on the basis of our own prejudices seems to be innate according to the findings of psychology. Think of Othello's tendency to confirm both to his image of himself, and of Iago, not to mention his image, or perhaps we should say, images of Desdemona.

On top of that, then, comes Othello's belief perseverance. Belief perseverance is the term to denote the human tendency to keep on believing what one has decided that one believes *a priori*, even in the face of disconfirming evidence. Hence the irony of his demand for 'ocular proof', 'Make me to see't' (III.3.369), and the use of the word 'see' in the line, 'Now do I see 'tis true' (III.3.449), because these fly in the face of his empiricist epistemology of, 'I'll see before I doubt, when I doubt, prove' (III.3.194).

Now the confirmation bias and belief perseverance are mutually reinforcing, and together as well as apart, they are thought of as possible solutions to, or ways of avoiding the unpleasant in case of our experiencing cognitive dissonance. That is the feeling of uncomfortable tension that comes from holding two conflicting thoughts in the mind at the same time – is Desdemona true or not? – which increases with the inability to rationalize and explain away this conflict. The idea is, that people try to arrive at consistency between what they do and what they believe, so inconsistency or dissonance will motivate a person to try to reduce the dissonance, and in trying so that person will actively avoid 'information which would likely increase the dissonance (Festinger 3)',[9] hence confirmation bias and belief perseverance. If we have acted on these, and the action has been completed and cannot be undone, then after-the-fact dissonance compels us to change our beliefs. That is of course exactly what happens with Othello in the final scene.

And then we haven't even begun to discuss the pitfalls and peculiarities of the processes of encoding, storage and retrieval of the information that a witness has, or the temporary blocking or permanent disappearance – transience of information –, for that matter. These are processes that we as professionals are called upon to interpret and judge, but from which we ourselves are not exempt. Sometimes we also misjudge what we see, or we miss part of the information before us. Biological and cognitive factors may cause illusions and delusions, and our expectations can lead to our seeing/witnessing stimuli that are not really 'out there'. And information can change, visual and verbal memory can as it were merge, the so-called 'verbal labeling-effect'.

One thing is certain, though. Karl Popper's falsification principle, thought essential for theory and practice, is definitely not encoded in our psychological make-up. In this sense, we would do well to remember Francis Bacon's admonition that, 'The human understanding is no dry light, but receives an infusion from the will and affections; whence proceed sciences which may be called 'sciences as one would wish'. For what a man had rather were true he readily believes.'[10] Bacon's legacy to lawyers is also the 'theory' of the Idols, i.e. mistaken ideas and methods, which have held men back from the truth. For our purpose, Bacon's distinction between the Idols of the Tribe, *idola tribus*, i.e. the tendency, once an opinion has been formed, to adhere to it in the face of contrary evidence with the help of continual rationalizations, or rather, the mistaken ways of thought which arise from human nature as such, and the Idols of the Cave, *idola specus*, i.e. the errors peculiar to the individual, each in his own cave, which arise from a person's own personal traits, and rearing, as well as his surroundings, is most helpful, in that it teaches us that the lessons of a philosophical history of ideas are not to be disregarded when it comes to present-day legal practice.

The confirmation bias in combination with a form of belief perseverance entails a huge risk for judges. When they have read the file, it is the information of that file that will direct their attitude during a trial, during an oral hearing. Miscarriage of justice may be the result.

9. See also, for an application of the concept of cognitive dissonance to what judges do, Robert Cover's *Justice Accused, antislavery and the judicial process.*
10. From Francis Bacon's *The New Organon* (1620), taken as a motto by Perez Sagorin. *Francis Bacon.* Princeton: Princeton University Press, 1998.

Judges and dramatists are readers for the plot; they select the facts, and structure reality, be it fictional or not, with an eye to final answers or a probable story. With the psychological predisposition I mentioned, the dangers to legal/judicial emplotment are obvious.

In order to open up a perspective, by means of a second conclusion, on an antidote for lawyers' tunnel vision, I take John Keats's idea of 'negative capability' as my guiding principle.[11] Far from propagating an instrumentalist use of literature, I claim, and I hope not to disrupt my argument in the eyes of literary scholars, that *as a metaphor* for what it means to write (and be) a great work of literary art, the quality of 'negative capability' is normative for the way in which lawyers should treat their materials: Impartial, with full attention to the different aspects of a case, and without the inclination to come to a final stand very quickly. And in the sense claimed here, it points at least theoretically to a similarity between law and literature, in that it points to a grounding for the 'and' of *Law and Literature* by focusing the interdiscipline on a literary quality which is also normative for judgement in law. That is to say, Keats' view of the poet's ability to be 'in uncertainties' resembles that of an ideal judge who likewise needs to be open to contingency and ambiguity. As a method of judging, therefore, it is normative for the legal profession. Simultaneously, legal practice presupposes for the actual moment of persuasive argument, the basic willingness to suspend disbelief in the sense Coleridge pin-pointed it (Coleridge 6), i.e. an acceptance, if only for that moment, of the world portrayed by others in legal proceedings, before coming to a harmony of diverging points of view as a starting point for further argument, a *concordia discordantium* as it was called in the scholastic tradition before this degenerated into casuistry.[12] These are basic attitudes for our word-oriented sections of the population. In all this I proceed from the claim that professional *phronèsis* (or practical wisdom in the Aristotelian sense of the application of good judgment to human conduct) can only be brought to fruition if lawyers develop a sense for context and perspective.

11. Keats in a letter to his brothers, 21 December 1817, ' ... that is when man is capable of being in uncertainties, ... doubts, without any irritable reaching after fact and reason', in: Abrams, M.H. and others, eds. *The Norton Anthology of English Literature*, vol.2, (705).
12. The source is Cicero's 'harmony of the spheres' (*Somnium Scipionis* in *De Republica, London Heinemann The Loeb Classical Library 1970*); see also Gratian's *Decretum* (1140), Emil L. Richter and Emil Friedberg eds. Leizig, 1881. For an extensive discussion, see Jeanne Gaakeer, '(Con)temporary Law' (29-46). See also Wolfgang W. Holdheim, *Der Justizzirrtum als literarische Problematik*.

31

A disclaimer before an audience from the humanities is perhaps in order now. With my references to Keats and Coleridge I might get into the contentious area of literature as an unproblematic repository of the humane, or I might overemphasize the ethical aspects, disregarding literature's wider system of cultural significance. Such anxiety, I would say, would touch a sore spot in our scholarship, and an important interdisciplinary issue, methodological reserve on both sides of the divide, which would also be an interesting topic for further discussion.

Bibliography

Baldwin, William. *The Mirror for Magistrates*. 1559. Cambridge: Cambridge University Press 1960 (1938).

Burton, R. *The Anatomy of Melancholy*. Introduction by Holbrook Jackson. London and Toronto: Dent and Sons Ltd., Everyman's University Library 1931.

Coleridge, S.T. *Biographia Literaria*. Princeton and London: Routledge and Kegan Paul: 1983: vol.II.

Cover, Robert. *Justice Accused, antislavery and the judicial process*. New Haven: Princeton University Press 1975.

Ferri, Enrico. *I Delinqenti nell'arte* 1896. Translated into French by Eugène Laurent as *Les criminals dans l'art et la literature*. Paris: Felix Alcan 1897.

Festinger, L. *A Theory of Cognitive Dissonance*. Stanford, California: Stanford University Press 1957.

Fogan, Lance MD. 'The Neurology in Shakespeare'. Vol.46 *Archives of Neurology* August 1989: 922-924.

Furman,Yury, MD, M. Wolf, MD, and David S. Rosenfeld, MD. 'Shakespeare and sleep disorders', Vol 49 *Neurology* 1988: 1171-1172.

Gaakeer, Jeanne. '(Con)temporary Law' *European Journal Society for English Studies*. Routledge volume 11, no.1, April 2007: 29-46.

Goetz, Christopher G. , MD. 'Shakespeare in Charcot's Neurologic teaching'. *Archives of Neurology* vol 45 August 1988: 920-921.

Greenblatt, Stephen and Walter Cohen, Jean E. Howard, Katharine Eisaman Maus, eds. *The Norton Shakespeare*, based on the Oxford edition by S. Wells and G. Taylor eds. New York and London: W.W. Norton and Co., 1997.

Holdheim, W. Wolfgang. *Der Justizzirrtum als literarische Problematik*. Berlin: Walter de Gruyter & Co. 1969.

Keats, John. 'Letter to George and Thomas Keats, dated 21 December 1817'. In: Abrams, Meyer H., E. Talbot, Hallett Smith, Robert M. Adams, Samuel Holt, Monk Lawrence Lipking, George H. Ford, and David Daiches. *The Norton Anthology of English Literature*. Volume 2. New York: Norton 1974.

Todd,J. and K. Dewhurst. 'The Othello Syndrome: a study in the psychopathology of sexual jealousy', vol.122 *Journal of Nervous and Mental Disorder* no. 4 1955: 67-374.

The Menace of Venice

Or Reading and Performing
the Law in/of *The Merchant of Venice*

Leif Dahlberg

> *There's his period –*
> *To sheathe his knife in us. He is attached.*
> *Call him to present trial. If he may*
> *Find mercy in the law, 'tis his; if none,*
> *Let him not seek't of us.*
> *(William Shakespeare and John Fletcher,*
> All is True *(*Henry VIII*), I.ii.210-214)*

Introduction

The textual situation of William Shakespeare's *The Merchant of Venice* (1598) is unusually good compared with many of his other plays, since the three principal sources conform with each other and also presumably conform with the author's manuscript (rather than a prompt book).[1] Yet it is not easy to know how to read the text of the play, nor is it a simple matter to stage and perform it. Although the play is presented as a comedy both paratextually[2] and in most theatrical performances,[3] and contains plenty of

---

1. See the introduction to William Shakespeare, *The Merchant of Venice*, ed. John Russell Brown (1955) (London, Thomson Learning, 2003), pp. xiv-xx. All citations of and references to the text of the play are to this edition. Citations of and references to other plays by Shakespeare are to *The Complete Works. Compact Edition*, ed. S. Wells et al. (Oxford U.P. 1998).
2. The title page of the first Quarto edition (1600) reads: 'The most excellent / Historie of the *Merchant / of Venice.* / VVith the extreame crueltie of *Shylocke* the Iewe / towards the sayd Merchant, in cutting a iust pound of his flesh: and the obtaining of *Portia* / by the choyse of three / chests. [...]' On the running head of each page the title is both abbreviated and transformed: 'The comicall History of / the Merchant of Venice.' The second Quarto edition (1619) slightly amends the title to 'The Excellent History of the Merchant of Venice', but retains the running heads of the first Quarto. The Folio edi-

jest, good humour and verbal wit, the play also has darker sides. The ending of the trial scene in the fourth act in particular has been viewed by many critics as troubling and difficult to accommodate with our sense of a happy resolution.[4] However, I will argue that the play strongly conforms to the laws of genre and of comedy. The principal support for this claim is that the strengthening of community presented and enacted in *The Merchant of Venice* operates by way of social inclusion, whereas in tragedy the strengthening of social bonds typically would take the form of exclusion and/or symbolic sacrifice of the protagonist in the form of a victim or scapegoat.

The difficulty of 'reading aright' is itself a recurring topos in the play, connected with the reading of character (Antonio's, but also the suitors' and Shylock's), executing a will (the will of Portia's dead father), solving riddles (the texts on the three caskets), reading legal documents (the bond and Venetian law), but also more generally with perceiving and understanding the difference between appearance and reality. In fact, one could argue that one of the central issues of the play is about the fate of reading. It should also be noted that the figure of reading appears in other, less topicalized places in the play, as when Lorenzo reads a letter in Jessica's 'fair hand' (II.iv.12), when Bassanio (in Belmont) reads Antonio's letter (III.ii.314-320),[5] and when the

tion (1623) has simply the 'The Merchant of Venice'. The published adaption of George Granville (Lord Lansdowne) from 1701 uses an alternative title, 'The Jew of Venice. A Comedy', which may have as its source either the 1598 record in the Stationer's Register: 'a booke of the Marchaunt of Venyce or otherwise called the Iewe of Venyce'.

3. Linda Rozmovits describes how *The Merchant of Venice* under Henry Irving's direction (1879) was transformed into a tragedy. See her *Shakespeare and the Politics of Culture in Late Victorian England* (62-63).

4. See for instance Nicholas Rowe, 'Some Account of the Life etc of Mr. William Shakespeare', in *Works*, 6 Vols. (1709), I, xix-xx, quoted in R.F. Hill, '*The Merchant of Venice* and the Pattern of Romantic Comedy' (75); W.H. Auden, 'Brothers & Others' (221); Sarah Kofman, *Conversions. Le Marchand de Venise sous le signe de Saturne* (68-69). Daniel Kornstein argues that although the play formally is a comedy, it should be termed a 'legal parable' (*Kill All the Lawyers? Shakespeare's Legal Appeal* (88-89)).

5. Antonio's letter (read by Bassanio): '*Sweet Bassanio, my ships have all miscarried, my creditors grow cruel, my estate is very low, my bond to the Jew is forfeit, and (since in paying it, it is impossible I should live), all debts are clear'd between you and I, if I might but see you at my death: notwithstanding, use your pleasure, – if your love do not persuade you to come, let not my letter.*' (III.ii)

Duke (in the court of justice in Venice) reads the letter from Bellario recommending Balthazar (IV.i.150-162).[6]

I will approach the question of reading – and of performing a reading – in and of the play by discussing in turn the problematics of reading Antonio's character, the execution of the will of Portia's father, the reading and solving of the riddles of the three caskets and choosing the right one, the reading of the bond between Shylock and Antonio both in terms of contract (civil law) and criminal act (criminal law). This will open the way for a critical discussion of how to read the terms 'Christian' and 'Jew' in the play, and also of the meaning of the double conversion enacted in the play, which is the most difficult part of the play to appreciate for a modern audience. In this way I will try to both enact and problematize the law of genre in and of the play.

Plot construction and place

Before we venture on this reading exercise, it is necessary to present the plot lines and to sketch the geography or topography of the play. The play has a double plot – the romance plot with Bassanio and Portia as main characters, and the bond/revenge plot with Antonio and Shylock as protagonists – that Shakespeare took over from his probable primary source, the first story of the fourth day in Ser Giovanni's *Il Pecorone*.[7] To this story Shakespeare has added both the casket scenes (which replaces the three journeys to Belmont in *Il Pecorone*) and the Lorenzo-Jessica sub-plot. The two main plots are interlaced in the play according to a regular and logical pattern so that, for instance, complications in the romance plot in the first act naturally motivate and lead over to the bond/revenge plot where Antonio secures Bassanio's romantic venture; and when in the third act it is revealed that Antonio's own

---

6. Bellario's letter (read by the Duke): '*Your grace shall understand, that at the receipt of your letter I am very sick, but in the instant that your messenger came, in loving visitation with me was a young doctor of Rome, his name is Balthazar: I acquainted him with the cause in controversy between the Jew and Antonio the merchant, we turn'd o'er many books together, he is furnished with my opinion, which (bettered with his own learning, the greatness whereof I cannot enough commend), comes with him at my importunity, to fill up your grace's request in my stead. I beseech you let his lack of years be no impediment to let him lack a reverend estimation, for I never knew so young a body with so old a head: I leave him to your gracious acceptance, whose trial shall be better publish his commendation.*' (IV.ii)
7. Ser Giovanni's *Il Pecorone* was written (in Italian) in the late 14th century and first printed in Milano in 1558.

ventures 'have miscarried', this inversely motivates Portia's intervention in the bond/revenge plot in the fourth act in order to rescue Antonio.[8]

In a similar way, the play moves between the two locations Venice and Belmont in a regular back-and-forth motion in the first three acts, whereas the fourth act entirely takes place in Venice (primarily in the court of justice) and the fifth act brings the story back to Belmont.[9] The movements between these

8. The interlacing of the plots can be graphically represented in the following diagramme:

Time	Plot 1 (Romance plot)	Plot 2 (Bond/revenge plot)	Sub-plot (Lorenzo-Jessica)
Act 1, scene 1	X	(X)	
Act 1, scene 2	X		
Act 1, scene 3		X	
Act 2, scene 1	X		
Act 2, scene 2			(X)
Act 2, scene 3			X
Act 2, scene 4			X
Act 2, scene 5		X	
Act 2, scene 6			X
Act 2, scene 7	X		
Act 2, scene 8		(X)	(X)
Act 2, scene 9	X		
Act 3, scene 1		X	
Act 3, scene 2	X		
Act 3, scene 3		X	
Act 3, scene 4	X	X	X
Act 3, scene 5			X
Act 4, scene 1		X	
Act 4, scene 2	(X)	X	
Act 5, scene 1	X		X

9. The movements between Venice and Belmont are represented in the following diagramme:

Time	Place 1 (Venice)	Place 2 (Belmont)
Act 1, scene 1	X	
Act 1, scene 2		X
Act 1, scene 3	X	
Act 2, scene 1		X
Act 2, scene 2	X	
Act 2, scene 3	X	
Act 2, scene 4	X	
Act 2, scene 5	X	
Act 2, scene 6	X	
Act 2, scene 7		X
Act 2, scene 8	X	
Act 2, scene 9		X
Act 3, scene 1	X	

locations – which takes place on water – are not represented in the play and neither is the time it takes to travel. In fact, although time in some respects is crucial for the interlacing of the plots (Shylock's loan to Antonio is for three months), the representation of time is neither realistic nor well measured, but rather indicates the order of events.[10] Another way of perceiving the absence of travel time in the play is to say that Venice and Belmont are floating on water (which in a way is factually true of Venice): At times they appear separate and distant, at other times adjacent and connected. In contrast to the minor role played by time in the play, the construction and production of place is of utmost importance.

The first thing to notice about the construction of place is the apparent differences and contrasts between the city of Venice and the (seemingly) rural Belmont (Tennenhouse 198-202). Whereas Venice appears to be a place for (male) friendship, commerce and positive law, Belmont is the realm of love, romance, and patriarchal law (law of the father). Venice is furthermore characterized by trade economy and capitalism, whereas the economy of Belmont appears to be based rather on agriculture and landed property. Venice is a place of heterogeneity and conflict, whereas Belmont is a place of homogeneity, harmony and music. Venice represents modern, urban reality, whereas Belmont is a foreign and perhaps even imaginary place, representing both past times and a possible happier future. Whereas Venice is a place for the regulated – but also irregular – use of (male) force, Belmont is a place where the strict (but virtuous) rule of patriarchal law appears open to subtle (female) manipulation. Although the two locations in these (and other) respects are constructed as each other's opposites, it is possible to move between them – though for women the transition should be made in male disguise – making the differences more nuanced and the contrasts less absolute. The transition

Act 3, scene 2		X
Act 3, scene 3	X	
Act 3, scene 4		X
Act 3, scene 5		X
Act 4, scene 1	X	
Act 4, scene 2	X	
Act 5, scene 1		X

10. For example, Bassanio has been in Belmont less than 24 hours, when a messenger arrives to announce not only that Antonio's ships are wrecked, but also that the time period of the loan (three months) has passed and that the loan is forfeit (III.ii.219f.); similarly, Lorenzo and Jessica appear to travel around in Italy with the speed of modern day transportation (III.i.72-120).

between the two places also involves an element of risk, since in the play water, apart from serving as a means of transportation, signifies danger.

The second thing to note about the construction of place in the play is that there are a number of correspondences between the two realms. Although Venice appears to be a place marked by risk and the need for financial security, in the stable agricultural economy of Belmont the will of the father sets up a veritable 'lottery' where Portia neither can choose between her suitors nor refuse anyone of them. In the play, the risk characteristic of Venice therefore corresponds to chance in Belmont. In this way Venice and Belmont at times appear not so much as separate and opposite, but as connected and even folded into each other. Related to the logic of contrast and correspondence between Venice and Belmont are the analogies with Elizabethan London and the English countryside, where you on the one hand find an urban economy based on trade and venture capital (corresponding to Venice) and on the other a rural economy based on agriculture and landed property (corresponding to Belmont), as well as growing conflicts between these economies. These analogies may be set up in the following matrix:

	'There'	*'Here'*
Urban (etc)	Venice (diegetic)	London
Rural (etc)	Belmont (diegetic)	English countryside

The representation of the opposition between Venice and Belmont on the Elizabethan theatrical stage hence has the function of ideologising the opposition and conflict between town and country, between trade economy and agricultural economy, etc. In this respect one may compare Shakespeare's Venetian comedy with the *fabula palliata*, which is the name given to the adaptations of Greek comedies on the Roman stage (its literal meaning is 'play in Greek dress'). The *fabula palliata* of Plautus and Terence simultaneously presented a distant and exotic reality (Greece) and represented local (Latin) moral problems in an 'other place' (heterotopia) where all similarities to real people, locations and events are accidental or coincidental. This way of constructing the diegetic space and place is of course also found in Shakespeare's other Italian plays – *The Two Gentlemen of Verona* (1580's), *The Most Excellent and Lamentable Tragedy of Romeo and Juliet* (1594-95) and *The Tragedy of Othello, the Moor of Venice* (1604) – and in his other plays situated in faraway places or distant times.[11] In this way one can say of Shakespeare's plays in general and of *The Merchant of Venice* in particular, that by simultaneously representing foreign countries and peoples and representing contemporary English society, it was possible both to superimpose and blend these realms ('here' and 'there') and to comment on them indiscriminately. Hence, in a similar way in which Venice and Belmont at times are made to connect and fold into each other in the play, the foreign places represented in the play are enfolded by the theatrical representation. The representations of 'here' and 'there' simultaneously implicate and complicate each other in ways reminiscent of representations and understanding of space in Baroque art and philosophy (Deleuze 38-54).

It has often been suggested that the legal proceedings in the play are informed by local (English) affairs, such as the trial and public execution of the Portuguese Jew Roderigo Lopez in London in 1594[12] – an event that is said to have spurred the restaging of Christopher Marlowe's *The Jew of Malta* (1589), a play that contains additional source material for Shakespeare's play (Shapiro 184-87 *et passim*). It has been argued, furthermore, that the legal proceedings in the play are informed by the historical and in Shakespeare's own time aggravated conflict between the traditional and independent common law system and the Court of Chancery.[13] The Court of Chancery constituted a court of appeal that tried the equity or fairness of sentences (but not questions of guilt). However, the Court of Chancery was also closer to the royal court and the perceived conflict between the rigidity of positive law and equity may to some extent be seen as a political struggle over control over the legal system. Although the correspondences with local events in England are suggestive and in some ways appear convincing, it is important to stress that

11. For an interesting discussion of the 'meaning' of Venice in Shakespeare's *The Tragedy of Othello, the Moor of Venice*, see Peter G. Platt, ''The Meruailous Site': Shakespeare, Venice and Paradoxical Stages' (121-154).

12. The connection between Shylock and the legal case of the Jewish physician Roderigo Lopez was first made by Sidney Lee in the article 'The Original of Shylock'. See Richard Halpern, *Shakespeare among the Moderns*.

13. See e.g. Mark Edwin Andrews, *Law versus Equity in The Merchant of Venice. A Legalization of Act IV, Scene I* ; George W. Keeton, *Shakepeare's Legal and Political Background*; O. Hood Phillips, *Shakespeare and the Lawyers;* Nicholas W. Knight, *Shakespeare's Hidden Life: Shakespeare at the Law* (178-190, 280-286); Theodore Ziolkowski, *The Mirror of Justice* (168-172). For attempts to apply the distinction between positive law and equity to the present times, see e.g. Kornstein, *Kill All the Lawyers?* (83-85 *et passim*); Daniela Carpi, 'Law, Discretion, Equity in *The Merchant of Venice* and *Measure for Measure*' (2317-2329).

they may be as obfuscated as the representation of Venice in the play. In Shakespeare and John Fletcher's play *All is True* (*Henry VIII*) (1613), great liberties are taken with recent English history (Wegemer 73-90). In other words, perceived similarities with historical and local events and with legal affairs in England are not sufficient in themselves to establish factual or causal relations with diegetic elements.

Furthermore, the interweaving and implication of Venice and London may not always have been intentional, but may also be due to lack of knowledge of actual Venice, both among the audience and in the writer. It should not be surprising, then, that since there were only a limited number of Jews in London in Shakespeare's time and their abodes and movements were not regulated by law as they were in historical Venice, there is no mention in the play of the regulations that governed that Jews in Venice were to remain in their ghetto after sundown (nor is there any mention of the ghetto in the play) and it is possible for the Jew Shylock to be invited to Bassanio's house for dinner (I.iii; II.v).[14] In a similar way, although in historical Venice the Doge had not presided over criminal proceedings since the 14th century (and magnificoes did not act as judges), in Shakespeare's play the 'Duke' is both present at the court of justice and presiding over the proceedings (IV.i). There are also occasional inconsistencies in the play, for instance that the sovereign city state of Venice is described both as a 'state' (III.iii.29) and as a town with a 'charter' that may be revoked (IV.i.39).

Here I would like to make a note on the construction of place when staging the play in later times and in other places – for instance in contemporary Stockholm – creating a double-layered 'there' according to the following matrix:

	'There' (1)	*'There' (2)*	*'Here'*
Urban (etc)	Venice (diegetic)	Elizabethan London	Stockholm
Rural (etc)	Belmont (diegetic)	Elizabethan countryside	Swedish countryside

The second or intermediary 'There' is not represented on stage (although it could be represented in the form of an Elizabethan stage), but rather serves as a mirror of or point of perspective on Venice. In other words, the audience

14. See Riccardo Calimani, *Histoire du ghetto de Venise*. For a critical discussion of the presence of Jews in England in Shakespeare's time, see James Shapiro, *Shakespeare and the Jews* (13-88).

should be well aware that the representation of Venice in the play is tainted by Elizabethan worldviews and that the presentation of actions and persons is governed by the theatre conventions of Shakespeare's time, and so on. This may be seen as a refraction or as another fold in the representation of the play. Likewise, contemporary stagings of the play may want to stress the distance to Elizabethan views by adding new elements to the plot. For instance, in a recent mise en scène of the play at the Royal Dramatic Theatre in Stockholm (2004), the trial scene in the fourth act contained a supplement in which the conversion of Shylock was staged.[15] However, the conversion was not presented as a joyful and socially inclusive event, but as a degrading and humiliating act.

This refraction or folding of representational space can be enacted yet another time in film adaptations of the play. For instance, in the film adaptation by Michael Radford (2004), there is, in contrast to the text of the play, an explicit and topicalized mention and representation of the Jewish ghetto in Venice, which creates a sub-place within the urban space. Although this is an addition to the play much like the conversion scene just mentioned, it can also be seen as a correction of the unhistorical representation of Venice in Shakespeare's play. The spatial matrix of this film adaptation would look something like this:

	'There' (1)	'There' (2)	'There' (3)	'Here'
Urban (etc)	Venice (diegetic) Jewish ghetto (diegetic)	Elizabethan London	Contemporary metropolitan USA ('Hollywood')	Stockholm
Rural (etc)	Belmont (diegetic)	Elizabethan countryside	Rural USA	Swedish countryside

Depending on what value one would understand as invested in the third 'There', the ideological construction of space and place will be quite different. The insertion of the Jewish ghetto in the diegesis together with the explicit show of anti-semitism (neither of which is found in the play) are in any case not innocent amendments. It is not obvious where to situate the ghetto in the matrix: Does it belong to the diegesis (There (1)) or to the representation

15. *Köpmannen i Venedig*, directed by Mats Ek, Royal Dramatic Theatre, Stockholm, 2004.

(There (3))? Perhaps it should be placed in the space created by folding the different 'Theres' into each other?

Although I have presented the construction of space in and of the play in terms of folds – both in the diegesis and in the staging – it should be noted that in the text of the play, the making of space is often a function of turning: Both literally in terms of 'turning' and figuratively as turns of phrase. We will return to these matrices, folds, and turns in the concluding discussion. But now, after having presented the plot and the construction of diegetic place and discursive space, it is time to try to read the script.

Reading in Venice

The text of the play – though not necessarily the play itself[16] – begins by Antonio speaking of his unexplainable 'want-wit sadness' that wearies both himself and his friends. Both Salerio and Solanio offer suggestions of how he has 'caught it, found it, or came by it' (I.i.3), but these are all refused by Antonio. Although it appears to be a recent affliction rather than a 'humour' in the sense of a character trait or medical diagnosis, Antonio professes to Bassanio that it is a more permanent condition: He famously says that the world is but a 'stage, where every man must play a part, / And mine a sad one.' (I.i.78-79). In response to this Gratiano suggests that it should be his own role to 'play the fool' (I.i.79). Gratiano certainly is both a merry and talkative character in the play, but the role of the fool or clown – an obligatory character in Elizabethan comedy (Wiggins 63, 70) – is played by Launcelot. However, when Antonio and Bassanio are left alone on the stage, Antonio immediately asks about the lady that Bassanio has 'sworn a secret pilgrimage' (I.i.119), and the reader is made to believe that it may indeed be this venture that is the cause of Antonio's sadness (Patterson 9-32). Regardless of the nature of Antonio's sadness and its possible causes, more significant in the play

---

16. In many stagings of the play one find an elaborate presentation of the city of Venice, as mentioned by John Russell Brown in his introduction to the Arden edition (pp. xxxiv). This is also the case in the recent film adaption by Michael Radford (2004), which begins by depicting the city as strongly anti-semitic (voice over) and in a scene on the Rialto is shown how Antonio unprovoked spits on Shylock. But it is not only the beginning of the play that may be transformed: in a discussion of 19th century representations of the play, Linda Rozmovits describes how on some occasions the play ended with the closing of the trial in the fourth act, leaving Shylock alone on the stage. See her *Shakespeare and the Politics of Culture in Late Victorian England* (78).

is the importance placed on 'knowing' oneself and revealing one's true character. This is indeed the central issue in the trial of character that the riddles of the three caskets perform on Portia's suitors.

The will or testament of Portia's dead father is first introduced in the play in the second scene of the first act by Portia herself in connection with a discussion of the difficulty of following good council:

> If to do were as easy as to know what were good to do,
> chapels had been churches, and poor men's cottages
> princes' palaces, – it is a good divine that follows his
> own instructions, – I can easier teach twenty what
> were good to be done, than be one of the twenty to
> follow mine own teaching: the brain may devise laws
> for the blood, but a hot temper leaps o'er a cold
> decree, – such a hare is madness the youth, to skip
> o'er the meshes of good counsel the cripple; but this
> reasoning is not in the fashion to choose me a hus-
> band, – O me the word 'choose'! I may neither
> choose who I would, nor refuse who I dislike, so is the
> will of a living daughter curb'd by the will of a dead
> father: [...] (I.ii.12-25)

What Portia says here is indeed true for most of us – it is all too easy to disregard both good council and one's own better judgment when the mind is tempted by what it desires – but it is not for Portia to choose by her own will, she must follow the will of her dead father. In his testament he has devised a sophisticated machinery that will ensure the selection of a true husband for his daughter. It consists of 'three chests of gold, silver, and lead' (I.ii.29-30) and the suitor 'who chooses his meaning chooses' Portia (I.ii.30-31). To Nerissa, Portia's maid, this deontological system appears more as 'lott'ry' (I.ii.28) than as good sense, but as is revealed in the second act, each chest or casket is provided with a verse that suggests its content and reveals the character of the 'chooser' (II.vii). Hence, when the suitors read and interpret the riddles of the caskets, they are as much reading as being read, and in performing a choice of one casket they are revealing their own true character. The reward promised by choosing the father's 'meaning' is to find Portia's portrait – as well as possessing the original. The punishment for not reading aright and choosing the wrong 'meaning' is either a carrion (the figure of vanity) or a fools head – and each of these are provided with verses that relay their meaning – but also to fulfill the promise not to woo another woman.

It is certainly called for to ask what it means to read the verses and to choose between the caskets. Is there indeed a 'right' reading and a 'right' choice? Is there an explicit rule that one may follow and that determines the right choice? Perhaps all choices are equally 'right' in that they reveal the truth of the suitor's character? And the issue would then not so much be a question of finding Portia's portrait but of knowing oneself and of knowing if one is (or will be) a good husband for Portia. In other words, we would find the same issue in the casket scenes as in the opening of the play, when we found Antonio having 'much ado to know' himself (I.i.7). One should also note that these tests of character are indeed obligatory ingredients in the traditional romance plot, where it is necessary to exhibit both the virtue of love and the love of virtue.[17] But the insistence on character and on virtue in the romance plot carries over to the other plot line in the play, and in the same way as Antonio and Bassanio (among others) have had their true characters read and tested, so will Shylock's character be read and tested in the trial in the fourth act.

I will not dwell on the readings that the princes of Arragon and Morocco perform of the verses and how they reveal their characters. They are after all minor figures in the play. There is reason, however, to tarry a little on Bassanio's performance and on his character. It has often been noted that although Bassanio in comparison with the princes is neither vain nor a fool, he is not really presented as a catch for Portia nor as an ideal male heir for Belmont. However, as Filomena Mesquita points out, Bassanio does personify the ideal of venture capitalism: Using other people's money for his own ends.[18] Hence the marriage between Bassanio and Portia signifies the fruitful union of trade economy and agricultural economy.

In his interpretation of the riddle, Bassanio shows proof of good judgment not only in discerning appearance and reality (III.ii.73-105), but also insight into the workings of the law:

> The world is still deceiv'd with ornament,
> In law, what plea so tainted and corrupt,
> But being season'd with gracious voice,
> Obscures the show of evil?
> (III.ii.73-77)

17. Whereas in the romance plot the virtue of love and the love of virtue are equally true and confirm each other, in the epic – a more serious literary genre – they are frequently opposed chiastically. For instance, in Virgil's *Aenid* Aeneas proves his virtue (*pietas*) by giving up his love for Dido.
18. See Filomena Mesquita, 'Travesties of Justice: Portia in the Courtroom' (122).

Within the context of the play, and in particular in relation to the trial scene in the fourth act, these lines can take on an ambiguous meaning either as a prolepsis of Shylock's use of the bond to get revenge on Antonio or as undermining Portia's graceful and technical legal argumentation – or both.

In contrast to the three riddles on the caskets and the verses inside them, the reader is not given the opportunity to read the bond between Antonio and Shylock. Instead we are offered a number of contesting and conflicting interpretations of its meaning and value. The primary meaning is that it is a contract stipulating the terms for Antonio's loan of three thousand ducats for three months from Shylock. In contrast to his usual habit, Shylock agrees to lend the money 'gratis', that is without interest. The suggested meaning of this in the play is that one lends money to friends without interest but to strangers and enemies with interest. Since Antonio and Shylock are anything but friends, it would seem natural for Shylock to take interest, but instead he offers a loan without interest as an offer of friendship to Antonio. The sincerity of this offer is strongly questionable, both in regard to Shylock's aside upon the entry of Antonio (I.iii.36-47) and in view of Antonio's previous hostile behaviour towards Shylock and other Jews (I.iii.101-124). Similarly one may question what it means that Antonio seemingly accepts this gesture of friendship and says not only that 'there is much kindness in the Jew' (I.iii.149), but speaks of Shylock as a 'gentle Jew. / The Hebrew will turn Christian, he grows kind.' (I.iii.173-174) One should remember that Antonio has said that he would 'call thee [a dog] again, / To spet on thee again, to spurn thee too.' (I.iii.125-126). But disregarding the sincerity of their gestures of friendship, this is the 'meaning' of the act of lending money without interest given in the play. It would be intriguing to pursue the role of friendship in this and other plays by Shakespeare, but I will have to leave that for another occasion.

It is equally open for questioning that the stipulation in the contract that 'the forfeit / Be nominated for an equal pound / Of your fair flesh, to be cut off and taken / In what part of your body pleaseth me' (I.iii. 144-147) is said to be a 'merry sport' (I.iii.141) – and hence not meant to be taken literally (Kornstein 72).[19] Indeed, Bassanio immediately protests against Antonio signing such a bond. In other words, the meaning of the bond in the play is uncertain already before it has been signed. But the uncertainty of its meaning

---

19. For a suggestive reading of the meaning of 'an equal pound / Of fair flesh', see James Shapiro, *Shakespeare and the Jews* (113-128).

troubles Antonio little since he expects to receive 'thrice three times the value of this bond' (I.i.155) a month before the forfeiture.

It is only when all his ventures have miscarried that the meaning of the bond becomes a serious issue for Antonio and indeed in the play itself, and it is only then that the issue of literal meaning and legal readings will arise. In the academic literature on the play there has been a long debate about the (positive) legal value of this bond, and one often find cited reference to the ancient Roman law (the Law of the Twelve Tables) that creditors could under certain circumstances divide the body of a debtor among themselves, but already Hegel noted that there is no historical evidence that this law ever was enacted (Hegel 26). One may also note that there are equally ancient laws that prohibit signing a contract that constitutes a threat to one's person or personal freedom.[20] As has already been mentioned, there are critics (both legal and literary) that want to place the play in the legal situation of Elizabethan England. It could also be mentioned that there have been many attempts to situate – or even retry – the case in modern legal systems (Tiefenbrun 149-235). On the question of the relevance of positive law, either Venetian or English, either ancient, early modern or modern, I would side with those who argue that it is not possible to judge or evaluate the events in the play based on historical law, whether canonical or secular, or other legal systems. However, the play certainly is informed by historical law and contemporary legal praxis, by conceptions of old law and new law (Hebrew and Christian law), as well as by thinking about natural law, and perhaps also that the play makes comments on the nature of law (White 159-184). This does not necessarily mean that law and legal proceedings in the play are to be seen as literary and the justice of the play is poetic justice. Rather, what it means is that we cannot simply short-cut the argumentation by saying that since the bond in the real world would be illegal and invalid, it would neither automatically nor necessarily imply that the bond is illegal or invalid in the play.

The first reading of the bond presented in the play is that of Shylock, whose desire for revenge has been maddened by anger at the loss of his daughter and of his ducats, and who argues that the 'merry sport' should be read literally.[21] The second reading is that of the Duke, who expresses his hope that Shylock will 'show [...] mercy' (IV.i.20) and withdraw his plea and 'Forgive a moiety of the principal' (IV.i.26). The third reading is that of

---

20. For instance in Solon's *seisachtheia* ('removal of burden'), as described in Aristotle, *The Athenian Constitution*, 6.
21. For a discussion of representations of revenge in Elizabethan drama, see Ronald Broude, 'Revenge and Revenge Tragedy in Renaissance England' (38-58).

Portia (appearing in the guise of man and with the symbolical name Balthazar),[22] who first maintains that the bond indeed is legally valid, but that there is another 'law' which demands of us to show mercy. The fourth reading is also performed by Portia: When Shylock has rejected the claim of mercy in this case, Portia on the one hand presents a hyper-literal reading of the bond – 'no jot of blood' (IV.i.302) – and on the other hand invokes the 'alien statute' of Venetian law and without notification turns the civil proceedings into a criminal trial (so called cross-action), accusing Shylock of having made an attempt on the life of a Venetian citizen. The penalty for this crime is execution by hanging.[23]

Although from a legal point of view it is quite reasonable to argue that the bond is invalid, this is not because it does not allow the letting of blood (that should be understood as part of taking flesh, since you can hardly take one without the other (Hecht 186-7, Colmo 319), but because it would be invalid (and therefore not legally binding) to sign a deed that constitutes a threat to one's own or somebody else's life (Hegel 73). It could also be argued, as has been done by several critics, that moving from one case to another is not according to due process, in particular moving from a civil case to a criminal case.[24] In other words, the court would have had to present a formal accusation that Shylock had made an attempt on Antonio's life, and allowed Shylock to defend himself against this allegation.[25] However, in Shakespeare's play the action moves directly from Portia's invalidation of the bond (which is a judgment in the civil proceedings) to the judgment that Shylock has tried to kill Antonio (which would be a judgment in a criminal trial). But since what is presented is not a real trial, one should not hasten to judge it by the same standards as in real life.

Moreover, the bond does not only have a literal legal meaning in the play. The bond between Antonio and Shylock can also be taken to signify the primordiality of contract in law, as the law of law, as well as the foundation for

22. Barbara Lewalski has argued that the name Balthazar contains an allusion to the Book of Daniel (where the prophet is called Balthazar). In the apocryphal Book of Susanna, the young Daniel – the name means 'the Judge of the Lord' – 'confounded the accusers of Susanna, upholding thereby the justice of the Law.' (Lewalski 340).

23. In historical Venice, the execution of death sentence followed an elaborate ritual, see Guido Ruggiero, *Violence in Early Renaissance Venice* (1-2 *et passim*).

24. See e.g. 'The Case of *The Merchant of Venice*: Shylock v. Antonio on appeal', in Susan Tiefenbrun, ed. (149-235).

25. An example from modern fiction film that illustrates this is Rob Reiner's *A Few Good Men* (1992). A similar move is found at the end of the film *The General's Daughter* (directed by Simon West, 1999).

civil society in a 'social contract.' In other words, the freedom to enter into voluntary and legally binding transactions is seen as fundamental to civil society.[26] In this way the bond can also be read as a symbol (an iteration) of social bonds between citizens. Hence, the invalidation of the bond in the play suggests, among other things, that the social bond uniting and constituting Venice is not so much a legal bond (a contract) as a moral bond, and that Shylock does not belong to this community until he has given up his bond and accepted the primacy of moral community over law.

I would suggest that when the tables are turned on Shylock, when the accuser becomes the accused, this is rather a figure – or a prefiguring – of the conversion that will be part of the sentence (or rather of the conditions for pardon). Not only are the civil proceedings converted to criminal proceedings, but the man who refused to give mercy to his enemy is forced to accept mercy by his new accusers. Before proceeding with this argument it is necessary to engage with the allegation that the mercy shown by the Court and by Antonio is hardly worth its name.

In order to save his life, Shylock not only has to give up all his property, he also has to give legitimacy to his daughter's union with Lorenzo, and finally also to convert to Christianity. Indeed, how could this sentence be considered 'mercy', let alone 'Christian' mercy? There have been voiced very strong opinions on this point, and many perceive that the talk of mercy is mere hypocrisy (Weisberg, 'Antonio's' 12-34). Thus, some critics have argued that the sentence is primarily ideological in that it allows the Christians to punish Shylock for pursuing an activity that their economic and financial system is dependent on, in other words using Shylock as a scapegoat.[27] It is hardly possible to seriously argue for the legality of the sentence and it is also difficult to argue what terms of mercy would be just in these circumstances. But in the poetic situation in the play, there is one bankrupt man, Antonio, whose life has been threatened by Shylock. In this respect it is not entirely unjust that part of the property of the one is given to the other as penance for having threatened his life. The fact that the property will be transferred to

---

26. Hegel objected strongly both to the idea of social contract as foundation of civil society and to the view that contract could be regarded 'als ein Vertrag aller mit allen, oder als ein Vertrag deiser aller mit dem Fürsten und der Regierung'. (80). See also the extended discussion of social contract in his *Über die wissenschaftlichen Behandlungsarten des Naturrechts* (1802-1803).
27. See A. D. Moody, 'The Letter of the Law (III.iii-v; IV.i)' (86); René Girard, 'To Entrap the Wisest. Sacrificial Ambivalence in *The Merchant of Venice* and *Richard III*' (243-255); Richard Halpern, *Shakespeare Among the Moderns* (176-184 *et passim*).

Lorenzo and Jessica at Shylock's death can both be seen as 'kind' and as a way of forcing Shylock to accept their union, including Jessica's (voluntary) conversion to Christianity.

However, the issue that appears to have provoked most critical controversy in recent times is the condition that Shylock must convert to Christianity lest the Duke should 'recant / The pardon that [he] late pronounced' (IV.i.387-388). Although it can be argued that a formal pardon may not be revoked – just as one may not 'unsign' documents or treaties once they have been signed[28] – what has disturbed both critics and audiences is the violence against the modern conception of freedom of religious creed as an inalienable human right.[29] In our secular times questions of religious faith tend to be considered to be private and a matter of personal choice, and it certainly would be offensive today to force religious conversion, especially under threat of death. But the situation is quite different both in the play and in Shakespeare's time. After all, the play is written some two hundred years prior to the French revolution and the declaration of universal human rights. One should also remember that in the view of Shakespeare's time, forcing Shylock to convert to Christianity not only made him part and member of the social body, it also enacted the salvation of his soul. But there is more in the conversion than meets the eye.

Reading conversion

As suggested already in the introduction, I would argue that the proper and legitimate mode of reading the conversion in the play – and also in Shakespeare's time – is as a figure of social inclusion rather than as a serious punishment or as a form of exclusion. It is possible to argue for this reading along several lines. Perhaps the most forceful argument – but to some extent a circular one – is to apply the law of genre. Although comedy may end by chastising and socially excluding the immoral personage – as in several of Molière's plays – , the 'meaning' of comedy in Shakespeare's time tended to be to reinforce social community by inclusion, not by exclusion. Hence we

28. See Edward T. Swaine, 'Unsigning'. See also Jim Lobe, 'Bush Mulls 'Unsigning' Treaty for International Criminal Court'; John B. Anderson, 'Unsigning the ICC'.
29. As formulated in the (French) Declaration of the Rights of Man and of the Citizen, article 10 (1789); the Constitution of the United States of America, first amendment (1791); the United Nations Universal Declaration of human rights (1948), article 18; the Charter of Fundamental Rights of the European Union, article 10 (2000).

find in the play the achievement of a union of men with women, of Venice with Belmont, and of the Jews with the Christians. Indeed, if Shylock's conversion was an actual punishment, it would imply a stigmatization. But in the context of the play, the conversion would inversely remove the markings of being an outsider.

Although this fits well with our understanding of a happy ending proper to comedy, there is also the issue of style and tone of the play, both in form and content. And indeed, the play mixes high and low elements (character, language, topics) in ways that befit classical comedy.[30] However, this aspect of comedy – which it shares with satire and (later) with the novel – has always been problematic for literary theorists that posit that one should not mix genres.[31] In the case of comedy it is not possible to define exactly what kind of elements belong to the genre or delimit a place in a system that belongs to it alone: Comedy is by definition a mixed genre – impure, parasitic, contaminated, inverted, invaginated (Derrida 237).[32] Rather, since comedy as a literary genre defines a certain mixture, a certain way of mixing elements, which may be found in narrative and drama as well as in film and interactive media, one may say of *The Merchant of Venice* that it participates in comedy without exclusively belonging to this genre. It is therefore not a violation of the genre to emphasize the more serious or darker sides in the play, as is done in several recent stagings and adaptations. In fact, the play may be said to participate in several genres, not all of which may be literary (Derrida 245). This inclusive schema is both an inherent part of comedy and part of the description of the genre – and it is natural that modern drama (Beaumarchais, Diderot, Büchner, Strindberg) develops from comedy and not from tragedy. As we will see, there is an analogy of sorts between the issue of literary genre and the question of religious and national identity.

At the time in history when Shakespeare lived and work, as James Shapiro has shown in an excellent study, both English national identity and Christian religious identity were being questioned and reconstructed (Shapiro 13-88). In the former case it was a response to changes in English society such as increasing mobility and trade, in the latter it was in response to the Reformation which divided the country. Obviously the two questions were intertwined. According to Shapiro, the question what is a Jew (or what makes a Jew a

---

30. Aristotle, *Poetics* (1447b24-48a27, 1449a33-37); see also the more extensive definition of tragedy at 1449b25-50a14.
31. Horace, *Ars poetica* (1-13); Nicolas Boileau-Despréaux, *Art poétique* (1674).
32. This implies that there is no single statute that governs or rules over genres. See Leif Dahlberg, *Tre romantiska berättelser* (325-361).

Jew) is the reverse (or mirror image) of the question what is an Englishman and a Christian. In other words, the issue of conversion has a peculiar meaning both in relation to these times of religious turmoil and in relation to a growing presence and awareness of foreigners. Although in Elizabethan England one had limited contact with and knowledge of Jews (converted or not), according to Shapiro there nevertheless existed an understanding that Jews, in contrast to other peoples, did not blend with or dissolve in other peoples (Shapiro 165-173). This may be contrasted with a conception of English self-identity common at the time, that the English constituted a mix of different peoples (Celts, Saxons, Normans, etc.) (Shapiro 43-45 *et passim*). It would appear, then, that the English were a mixed genre of people, albeit not always and not necessarily of a humorous kind.

The literal meaning of religious conversion is about turning to and following the 'right' path, but reading the conversion in the play is also a question of reading the terms 'Christian' and 'Jew', both in a historical context and in view of our own times. As just mentioned, the meanings of these terms were not fixed, but were being unsettled, questioned and reposited. The issue of forced conversion and persecution of Jews also take on a different meaning in relation to contemporary historical events in Portugal and Spain and in other places, and is also related to the persecution of other religious and ethnic groups (Shapiro 5-6, 14-20, 131-165). Without wanting to bracket or put aside these issues, I would like to venture on a reading of the conversion in the play as a rhetorical schema – a figure of thought – for solving legal and social conflicts and for conceiving community. In this light, conversion does not (or not only) signify a change of religious faith, turning from one religion to another, nor moving from one genre of belief to another. It is not a question of turning things about or inside-out (inversion) in ways that will change their nature (perversion). Rather, in conversion we meet a figure of turning around or turning-with, of 'with-turning', as in dance when one turns together with each other (and with the music). In *The Merchant of Venice*, the site of the conversion coincides with the place of law, and this spatial convergence suggests that the space of law in the play is defined by the conversion. In this light, the ultimate end or telos of a legal trial is neither punishment (or revenge) nor reconciliation between parties, but that the parties perceive or understand that there is a another ('higher') interest than their own particular or individual interests. In other words, conversion is a figure producing a certain legal space that shapes and defines the discursive activity of the courtroom, either virtual or real.

There are a number of questions that arise from this view of the conversion as producing a certain kind of legal space, but we can only touch upon a few of them here. First, the suggestion that legal court practice imitates the conceptual schema of religious conversion, should be simultaneously intriguing and disturbing for a legal system that tries to keep out the specter of religion from law – as any positivist legal system would – and this may in turn invite comparisons between how legal systems deal with those who do not conform to their standards and how religious institutions handle moral issues. Second, it invites questions regarding mediatisation and spectacle: Are legal trials to be considered as a primarily closed – even private – space or are they open and public? And what is the current understanding of 'public space' in law? If the legal space of the courtroom is defined by a certain closure and a highly limited access for media – which is the case in most Western societies today – then what is the meaning of the term open and public trial? In other words, where is the place of law in contemporary society? In what discursive and social folds do legal conversions take place?

A third series of questions concern the relation between society and the trial as a place of law. It is easy to see that the court of law represents society in the sense that it acts on behalf of society. However, the court of law also represents society as a re-presentation or image of society, and in this way it constitutes what Michel Foucault called a 'heterotopia', an 'other place' that constitutes society in providing us with a structural representation of society (Foucault 1571-1581). In what ways does the court of law constitute society in terms of the conversion? I believe one could view the legal conversion as the enactment or pronunciation of community in the sense that particular interests are articulated within the fold(s) of law. This should not be taken to mean that it is the individuals that constitutes the community, but obversely that it is the conversion that constitute them as singular members of a community. In this way the legal conversion could perhaps be seen as a version of what Jean-Luc Nancy calls the 'co-appearance' or 'com-pearence' (*comparaissance*) of the finitude of the singular being (Nancy 68-78). In other words, it is in the legal space of the conversion, enacted in the court of law, that the legal subject is made visible, becomes 'ex-posed', by the community. This line of thought obviously needs to be elaborated, but this is not the place for that venture.

It is time to conclude. Perhaps there is no other – or more proper – way to end but by returning to the scene of the conversion, which after all is not represented in the text of the play. It is imperative that we read and re-read this critical point, this turning point in the play. The meaning of the conversion is indeed the spinning movement that it sets in motion at the centre of the legal and theatrical stage.

Bibliography

Anderson, John B. 'Unsigning the ICC', *The Nation*, April 29 2002 <http://www.thenation.com/ doc/20020429/anderson>.

Andrews, Mark Edwin. *Law versus Equity in The Merchant of Venice. A Legalization of Act IV, Scene I.* Boulder: Univ. of Colorado Pr. 1965.

Arneson, Richard J. 'Shakespeare and the Jewish Question'. *Political Theory*, Vol. 13, No. 1, February 1985: 85-111.

Auden, W.H. 'Brothers & Others'. In *The Dyer's Hand and Other Essays*. New York: Random House 1963.

Barber, C.L. 'The Merchants and the Jews of Venice: Wealth's Communion and an Intruder'. In L.F. Dean, ed. *Shakespeare: Modern Essays in Criticism*. New York: Oxford U.P. 1967: 204-227.

Barnet, Sylvan, ed. *The Merchant of Venice. A Collection of Critical Essays* Englewood Cliff: Prentice-Hall 1970.

Benston, Alice N. 'Portia, the Law, and the Tripartite Structure of *The Merchant of Venice*'. In T. Wheeler, ed. *The Merchant of Venice. Critical Essays*. New York: Garland Publishing 1991: 163-194.

Bronstein, Herbert. 'Shakespeare, the Jews, and *The Merchant of Venice*'. *Shakespeare Quarterly*, Vol. 20, No. 1, Winter, 1969: 3-10.

Broude, Ronald. 'Revenge and Revenge Tragedy in Renaissance England'. *Renaissance Quarterly*, Vol. 28, No. 1, Spring, 1975: 38-58.

Brown, John Russell. 'Love's Wealth and the Judgment of *The Merchant of Venice*'. In Sylvan Barnet, ed. *Twentieth Century Interpretations of The Merchant of Venice*. Englewood Cliffs: Prentice Hall, 1970: 81-90.

Burckhardt, Sigurd. '*The Merchant of Venice*. The Gentle Bond'. *ELH* Vol. 29 No. 3 1962: 239-262.

Calimani, Riccardo. *Histoire du ghetto de Venise*, trad. S. Rotolo. Paris: Éd. Stock 1988.

Carpi, Daniela. 'Law, Discretion, Equity in *The Merchant of Venice* and *Measure for Measure*'. *Cardozo Law Review* May 2005: 2317-2329.

Colley, John Scott. 'Launcelot, Jacob, and Esau: Old and New Law in The Merchant of Venice'. In *Literature and Its Audience*, special number of *The Yearbook of English Studies*, Vol. 10 1980: 181-189.

Colmo, Christopher. 'Law and Love in Shakespeare's *The Merchant of Venice*'. *Oklahoma City University Law Review*, Vol. 26, No. 1 2001: 306-326.

Cooper, John R. 'Shylock's Humanity'. *Shakespeare Quarterly*, Vol. 21, No. 2 Spring, 1970: 117-124.

Dahlberg, Leif. *Tre romantiska berättelser.* Stockholm: Symposion 1999.

---. 'Rätt och retorik i Euripides *Hekabe*'. *Rhetorica Scandinavica* 39 2006: 34-52.

Deleuze, Gilles. *Le Pli. Leibniz et le Baroque*. Paris, Minuit 1988.

Derrida, Jacques. *Parages*, nouv. éd. augmentée. Paris: Ed. Galilée: 2003.

Echeruo, Michael J.C. 'Shylock and the 'Conditioned Imagination': A Reinterpretation'. *Shakespeare Quarterly*, Vol. 22, No. 1. Winter, 1971: 3-15.

Elster, Jon. 'Norms of Revenge'. *Ethics*, Vol. 100, No. 4 July 1990: 862-885.

Fletcher, John. *Valentinian*. In M. Wiggins, ed. *Four Jacobean Sex Tragedies.* Oxford: Oxford U.P. 1998.

Foucault, Michel. 'Des Espaces autres'. In Michel Foucault, *Dits et écrits II, 1976-1988*, ed. D. Defert & F. Ewald. Paris: Gallimard, 2001: 1571-1581.

Girard, René. *A Theater of Envy. William Shakespeare*. New York: Oxford U.P.1991.

Graham, Cary B. 'Standards of Value in *The Merchant of Venice*'. *Shakespeare Quarterly*, Vol. 4, No. 2 April, 1953: 145-151.

Gross, John. *Shylock. Four Hundred Years in the Life of a Legend*. London: Chatto & Windus 1992.

Halpern, Richard. *Shakespeare Among the Moderns*. Ithaca: Cornell U.P. 1997.

Hankey, Julie. 'Victorian Portias: Shakespeare's Borderline Heroine'. *Shakespeare Quarterly*, Vol. 45, No. 4 Winter 1994: 426-448.

Hecht, Anthony. *Obligati: Essays in Criticism*. New York: Atheneum 1986.

Hegel, G.W.F. *Grundlinien der Philosophie des Rechts*. Hrsg. J. Hoffmeister. Hamburg: Verl. Felix Meiner, 1955.

Hill, R.F. '*The Merchant of Venice* and the Pattern of Romantic Comedy', *Shakespeare Survey* 28 1975.

Hunter, G.K. *English Drama 1586-1642. The Age of Shakespeare. The Oxford History of English Literature VI*. Oxford: Clarendon Press 1997.

Keeton, George W. *Shakepeare's Legal and Political Background*. London: Pitman 1997.

Keevak, Michael. *Sexual Shakespeare. Forgery, Authorship, Portraiture*. Detroit: Wayne State U.P 2001.

Knight, Nicholas W. *Shakespeare's Hidden Life: Shakespeare at the Law*. New York: Mason & Lipscomb 1973.

Kofman, Sarah. *Conversions. Le Marchand de Venise sous le signe de Saturne*. Paris: Galilée 1987.

Kornstein, Daniel J. *Kill All the Lawyers? Shakespeare's Legal Appeal*. Princeton: Princeton U.P. 1994.

Lee, Sidney (1880). 'The Original of Shylock'. *Gentleman's Magazine* 268 January-June 1880: 185-200.

Lewalski, Barbara K. 'Biblical Allusion and Allegory in *The Merchant of Venice*'. *Shakespeare Quarterly*, Vol. 13, No. 3 Summer 1962: 327-343.

Lobe, Jim. 'Bush Mulls 'Unsigning' Treaty for International Criminal Court'. *OneWorld.net* 5 April 2002 <http://www.commondreams.org/headlines02/0405-02.htm>.

Lupton, Julia Reinhard. *Citizen-Saints. Shakespeare and Political Theology*. Chicago: Univ. of Chicago Pr. 2005.

Marston, John. *The Malcontent and Other Plays*. Ed. K. Sturgess. Oxford: Oxford U.P. 1997.

Martin, John & Dennis Romano, eds. *Venice Reconsidered. The History and Civilization of an Italian City-State, 1297-1797*. Baltimore: Johns Hopkins U.P. 2000.

Meron, Theodor. 'Crimes and Accountability in Shakespeare'. *The American Journal of International Law*, Vol. 92, No. 1 January, 1998: 1-40.

Mesquita, Filomena. 'Travesties of Justice: Portia in the Courtroom'. In *Shakespeare and the Law*. Ravenna: Longo Editore 2003: 117-125.

Moody, A.D. 'The Letter of the Law (III.iii-v; IV.i)'. In T. Wheeler, ed. *The Merchant of Venice. Critical Essays*. New York: Garland Publishing, 1991: 79-101.

Nancy, Jean-Luc. *La Communauté désœuvrée*. Paris: Bourgois 1986.

Norwich, John Julius. *A History of Venice*. London: Penguin Books 2003.

O'Rourke, James. 'Racism and Homophobia in *The Merchant of Venice*'. *ELH* Vol. 70 2003: 375-397.

Patterson, Steve. 'The Bankruptcy of Homoerotic Amity in Shakespeare's *Merchant of Venice'*. *Shakespeare Quarterly*, Vol. 50, No. 1 Spring 1999: 9-32.

Phillips, O. Hood. *Shakespeare and the Lawyers*. London: Methuen 1972.

Pilkington, Ace G. 'Shakespeare on the Big Screen, the Small Box, and in between'. In *Literature in the Modern Media: Radio, Film and Television*, special number of *The Yearbook of English Studies*, Vol. 20 1990: 65-81.

Platt, Peter G. ''The Meruailous Site': Shakespeare, Venice and Paradoxical Stages'. *Renaissance Quarterly*, Vol. 54. No. 1 Spring 2001: 121-154.

Pullan, Brian. *The Jews of Europe and the Inquisition of Venice, 1550-1670*. Oxford: Basil Blackwell1983.

Romano, Dennis. *Patricians and Popolani. The Social Foundations of the Venetian Renaissance State*. Baltimore: Johns Hopkins U.P. 1987.

Rozmovits, Linda. *Shakespeare and the Politics of Culture in Late Victorian England*. Baltimore: Johns Hopkins U.P.1998.

Ruggiero, Guido. *Violence in Early Renaissance Venice*. New Brunswick: Rutgers U.P. 1980.

Shakespeare, William. *The Complete Works. Compact Edition*. Ed. S. Wells et al. Oxford: Oxford U.P. 1998.

---. *The Merchant of Venice*. Ed. John Russell Brown. London: Thomson Learning 2003.

Shapiro, James. *Shakespeare and the Jews*. New York: Columbia U.P. 1996.

Swaine, Edward T. 'Unsigning'. *Stanford Law Review* May 2003.

Tennenhouse, Leonard. 'The Counterfeit order of *The Merchant of Venice'*. In T. Wheeler, ed. *The Merchant of Venice. Critical Essays*. New York: Garland Publishing 1991: 195-215.

Tiefenbrun, Susan, ed. *Law and the Arts*. Westport: Greenwood Press 1999.

Ward, Ian. *Shakespeare and the Legal Imagination.* London: Butterworths 1999.

Wegemer, Gerard B. 'Henry VIII on Trial: Confronting Malice and Conscience in Shakespeare's *All is True'*. In S.W. Smith & T. Curtright, eds. *Shakespeare's Last Plays. Essays in Literature and Politics*. Lanham: Lexington Books 2002: 73-90.

Weisberg, Richard H. *Poethics and other Strategies of Law and Literature*. New York: Columbia U.P. 1992.

---. 'Antonio's Legalistic Cruelty'. *College Literature* Vol. 25 No. 1 Winter 1998: 12-34.

Wheeler, Thomas, ed. *The Merchant of Venice. Critical Essays*. New York: Garland Publishing 1991.

White, R.S. *Natural Law in English Renaissance Literature*. Cambridge: Cambridge U.P. 1996.

Wiggins, Martin. *Shakespeare and the Drama of his Time*. Oxford: Oxford U.P. 2000.

Yaffe, Martin D. *Shylock and the Jewish Question*. Baltimore: Johns Hopkins U.P. 1997.

Ziolkowski, Theodore. *The Mirror of Justice.* Princeton: Princeton U.P. 1997.

Killing an Arab = ?

On Judgments as Literature and Literature as Judgment: Albert Camus' novel *L'étranger*

Arild Linneberg

> *'I'm alive*
> *I'm dead*
> *I'm the stranger*
> *Killing an Arab'*
> *(*The Cure*)*

The Mother, the Murder, the Sentence: Death

When I, for the first time, read Albert Camus' *L'étranger* – *The Stranger* – I did not like it, and I did not understand it – which according to the Norwegian poet and philosopher of rhetoric Georg Johannesen most often is one and the same thing: to like and to understand (59). But since then this novel has become one of the novels that I like the most. It is a very complex work of art; and in the study of literature and law *L'étranger* is a *must*. The novel not only deals with crime and punishment and the logic of justice and law, it also teaches the reader about law's stories and the construction of narratives in court; furthermore it tells about how to judge – and the structure of judicial opinions, and, especially, the novel deals with the question of capital punishment: the death sentence and death penalty.[1]

The opening paragraph of the novel immediately points to the main themes:

> Aujourd'hui, maman est morte. Ou peut-être hier, je ne sais pas. J'ai reçu un télégramme de l'asile 'Mère décédée. Enterrement demain. Sentiments distingués.' Cela ne veut rien dire. C'était peut-être hier. (Camus 9)

---

1. In my book *Tolv og en halv tale om litteratur og lov og rett* ('Twelve and a half Speeches on Literature and Law'), I give a more extensive reading of Camus' novel.

In English:

> Today mama died. Or maybe it was yesterday, I don't know. I got a
> telegram from the nursery home. 'Mother dead. Funeral tomorrow.
> Sincerely yours.' It does not matter. Maybe it was yesterday.[2]

What happens thereafter has always got me thinking of a verse line in a poem
of the Danish poet Per Højholt: 'en mor er et mord uten d'. The pun gets *lost
in translation* when translated into English; but the meaning is: 'a mother
(*mor*) is a murder (*mord*) without a d (the letter d)'. The death of his mother,
and the funeral and what follows turn out to be disastrous to Meursault. He is
sentenced to death because of a man slaughter – which he has actually also
committed. The mother and the murder are the points of departure for this
novel's discussion of literature and law.

The novel is structured in two parts. The first part deals with the incidents
taking place after his mother's death and ends with Meursault killing an
Arab. The second part tells the story of what happens to Meursault in prison,
deals with the inquiry – lasting for eleven months – the trial and the theater of
the court room, and finally gives an account of what Meursault is thinking before he is executed.

As the Norwegian author Dag Solstad once put it: A novel is a story that cannot be retold. Still, I will give a sketch of some incidents in *The Stranger*'s
story – because the relation between the two parts and the two stories of the
novel is essential for the novel's discussion of judicial opinions and legal narratives.

First, however, a few words about the novel's historical context, i.e. also
the historical actuality of Camus' work; the text deals with themes such as
terrorism and war. *The Stranger* was written in a context of – French – colonialism and imperialism and suppression in the third world, and with terrorism as an answer to the western world. In Algeria the first *muhajeddins* –
holy soldiers – began fighting against French colonialism using the method of
terrorist attacks. At a time when he was a member of the Communist Party,
Camus wrote in two leftist newspapers in Algeria, both of them were forbid-
den in 1940, and one year later, in 1941, he published an essay concerning
the political situation in Algeria and especially the situation of the extremely
poor Arab population. At the same time he started to write *The Stranger*,

2. All quotations translated from French into English, by Arild Linneberg.

which was published the year after, in 1942. (A side comment: 'Jean Mersault' was the pseudonym of Camus when he wrote his journalistic articles before the Second World War).

The conflict between the French colonialist world and the Arab world – in a situation where blind violence and terrorism were developing, is the concrete historical situation in which the novel was written and published. The problem of justice, judgments, law and the legal system in the novel – and the death penalty as treated by Camus, is closely connected to this historical and geopolitical situation.

Meursault: Man or 'Moral Monster' – the Law against Humanities

The novel's first sentence is 'Aujord'hui, maman est morte'. The first words in the telegram from the funeral home, were 'Mère décedée'. *Maman* and *mère* is not the same word. A difference and a conflict between Meursault and the public institutions are already here made apparent. This difference and this conflict are being developed through the two versions of the story about Meursault and the murder.

I will remind you of some details. The day before the funeral, Meursault rejects to see his mother's body in the coffin, and sitting by the coffin, he drinks a café au lait and also smokes a cigarette. At the funeral, he does not cry – neither does he remember his mother's age. After the funeral, he meets Marie, they go swimming and to watch a movie. Later we get acquainted with his comrade Raymond, we are told that he is helping Raymond, who has a disagreement with his girlfriend, and Meursault and Raymond feel somewhat threatened by some Arabs, who Raymond is somewhat afraid of because he has beaten his – Arab – girlfriend. On the afternoon the following day, they have lunch at Massons in a bungalow on the beach, and after lunch Meursault takes a walk alone on the beach, he discovers one of the Arabs behind a stone, gets sight of the Arab's knife gleaming in the sun, and he all of a sudden shoots him – with five shots, with the gun he has got from Raymond.

Some other episodes in the first part of the novel, also teach us about some aspects of Meursault's personality; such as him being friendly, being nice to his neighbour who has lost his dog, that he rejects to go to Paris for a better job and that he is an honest man, honest to himself and to Marie.

In the second part of the novel, the story about Meursault, his mother, his friends and the killing, is being retold. First the events before and after the murder are reconstructed by the investigator, then retold in court by the prosecutor and finally in the judge's judicial opinion. They all consider Meursault to be 'a moral monster', inhuman, strange to mankind, estranged from humanity.

It is this, the lawyers' narration of the story of Meursault in the second part of the novel, in relation to the story we as readers are being told in the first section, that lies at the heart of the novel.

This relation is complex, however, it concerns several aspects of Camus' investigation of law, the legal system and judicial opinions, of legal language – and, it seems to me, it contains all in all a fundamental criticism of the whole legal system's way of functioning.

According to Richard Weisberg, in *The Failure of the Word*, a major distinction between the legal traditions of the Continent and the traditions in the US, is 'the dramatic intent of narrative-oriented criminal procedure' in Europe: 'The European trial (...) is no more than a representation in dramatic and linguistic form of a view of the defendant created by the inquisitor from the data of the preliminary inquiry.' As Richard Weisberg sees it, Camus has realized this (*The Failure* 57).

How is this dramatic narration constructed? When the details from the novel's first part are being retold in the second – by the investigator, the prosecutor and the judge – every single detail changes its meaning. It is as if the law's story is an artistic technique similar to the *ostranenie – defamiliarization – estrangement* – of the story told in part one. The lawmen's reconstructions of the events, is characterized by what Viktor Shklovsky called 'semantic modifications'. With Michail Bakhtin's theory of the novel, we could say that the reconstruction in court of what actually happened – in the fiction's 'real world' – has a high degree of artistic novelness.[3] Or, to put it in other words, the law's narrations of the real in the novel's part two is shown to be 'fictitious' in relation to the 'factual' sequence of incidents told in part one.

The legal procedure's conclusion is, so Richard Weisberg, that Meursault is a 'moral monster', a conclusion 'that derives from the deliberate exaggeration of incidents which were wholly unrelated to the actual crime.'

In the verdict's judicial opinion Meursault is said to lack human feelings, among other things because he had not been crying at his mother's funeral. But in the first half part of the novel we, as I said, are being told that Meur-

---

3. See Arild Linneberg, 'Romanheten i sentrum: Mikhail Bakhtin, dialogens filosof', in Arild Linneberg *Tretten triste essays om krig og litteratur* (135-153).

sault has a highly sensitive character. The representatives of the law use against him that he smoked a cigarette, drank a cup of coffee, went swimming and to watch a movie with Marie closely before and after his mother's burial. But these incidents, on the contrary, can be said to show us that the protagonist is sensual of nature. The fact that he is so affected by the heat and the sun, underlines his sensitivity.

What else do we know about this 'moral monster'? He is kind to his neighbour. He is a good friend. Aristotle said: A friend is a person who is just to you. The Norwegian author Aksel Sandemose wrote: A friend is a person, who, when you have committed a murder, will help you to get rid of the body. Friendship is a third kind of love, Derrida says in his *Politics of Friendship*. But to the friends testifying for Meursault in court, the prosecutor and judge pay no attention.

It is as if Camus is saying, Meursault is human, the legal institution is not.

Meursault's honesty is clearly shown in his relationship to his girlfriend Marie. When she asks him if he loves her, he answers *no*. When she then asks whether he will marry her, his answer is *yes ok*! However, this honest man is also capable of saying phrases like: 'I'm sure I loved my mother, but that didn't mean anything. All healthy creatures have more or less desired the death of the people they love.'

The defendant is honest, the legal institution is not. The story created in part two by lawyers and judges is dishonest. The legal discourse is lying. Or, maybe, Camus is contrasting the law against humanities.

Two different languages – deconstructing each other
The difference between the two stories of what is supposed to be 'identical' events, demonstrates, to quote Paul Gewirtz in Peter Brooks' *Law's Stories –* 'how literature and law shape reality through language' (Brooks and Gewirtz 4). Meursault uses words quite sparingly, he is a quiet man, nearly nonverbal. The investigator wants him to recall and verbalize everything, and is also himself establishing a legal discourse in accordance with the rhetorical rules of legal language.

This legal discourse is obviously governed by an instrumental rationality, which Meursault explicitly opposes, when remaining silent, and for instance when he does not want to be promoted to a better job in Paris; to him life is good enough just the way it is, Meursault says.

What Camus sketches in *The Stranger*, is not only the two different stories. Through this text he analyzes the construction of false and fictitious narratives in court. He shows us two different types of language-constructed reality, two types of discourses involving two types of logic contradicting each other, and two apparent distinguished ethics, two different value systems, each of them opposing the other. *The Stranger* presents and represents what deconstruction is meant to be, how deconstruction operates in and between two different types of languages.

'Meursault had killed and deserved punishment, but the measure of punishment is caused less by Meursault's *intent* at the time of the homicide than by his morality in general', Richard Weisberg has written (*Poethics* 44). What does Meursault's 'morality in general' imply, what are the characteristics of this moral value system of his, as represented by his nonconformity, his way of communicating and his non-instrumental language and logic of thought – as opposed to the values of the law?

We can best answer by asking: What does the opposed value system represent; the morality and ethics of the law, as expressed in court, i. e. in the legal system? Why is Mersault condemned and convicted? The leader of the surrealistic movement in France, André Breton, wrote, in the first surrealistic *manifesto*, 1924: 'Down with the Family, the State and with Religion!' Without ever expressing it in words, Meursault represents a similar attitude. *First*, Meursault apparently showed insensitivity at his mother's funeral, meaning: He did and does not respect the family. According to the prosecutor, Meursault's attitude towards his old mother, proves that he is a 'father-killer'. *Second*, Meursault is not a Christian. The investigator calls him 'anti-Christ', in rage holding a crucifix up against Meursault's face. Meursault denounces both God and Christianity. *Third*, Meursault is sentenced to death 'in the name of the French nation' – and this is what the judge emphasizes. Meursault honestly denies the three main values: the family, religion and the nation-state. These are the three main reasons in the judicial decision for giving Meursault the death-sentence.

Literature as judgment
I have focused on the legal discourse as literature, as a dramatized narrative. The judicial opinion and the judgment are literary utterances. *The Stranger*, however, is, as literature, as a novel, also a judgment, judging the judgments of the judges; judging the law, the legal texts and the legal culture.

A main theme in *The Stranger* is the question of who and what the others and the other actually are. To answer this question, we must turn back into the novel's historical context: Algeria 1940, war, colonialism, and terrorism.

Meursault was sentenced to death for killing an Arab. The court, however, does not pay much attention to that. Why not? How much attention did the French pay to the Arabs, in Algeria? They killed, and tortured, thousands. In 1945 the French at one single occasion, killed approximately more than twenty thousand Algerians, maybe many more, who were rioting against the French occupation. This happened even before the Algerian War – wherein the French certainly also bombed with napalm and destroyed most of Algeria's prolific areas.

Meursault committed homicide in blindness, it was so-called blind violence, 'it was because of the sun!' He was convicted.

How many hundreds of thousands of poor Arabs did the French colonialists kill in Algeria? Without anyone anytime being brought to justice? This is not an unreasonable question, if Camus' novel itself is a *ratio decidendi* so to speak allegorically convicting the French legal system to a symbolic death for not having convicted those who should also have been convicted?

I shall end with some closing comments concerning *The Stranger* in relation to Frantz Fanon's *Les damnés de la terre*, 1961, and Albert Camus' own essay from 1955, entitled 'Reflections on the Guillotine'. Camus' essay was actually published in the first volume of texts concerning the 'Literature and Law'- movement, *The Law as Literature. An Anthology of Great Writing in and about the Law*, selected and introduced by Louis Blom-Cooper, 1961. How did the French look at the Algerian Arabs? A very well respected French psychiatrist and brain-researcher wrote in the 1930's: 'An African uses his brain very little. (...) In fact the normal African is like an European with a brain damage.' The French, however, also were afraid of these Arabs, these others: 'The typical Algerian is very often aggressive, he often kills and without reason – and mainly with the knife.' (Fanon 20-1)

Read in this context, Meursault appears in a new light. He is a French-Algerian. Killing an Arab does not seem to bother him: In this respect he was typically French. However, in murdering an Arab, Meursault is acting in accordance with the French view of the Algerians, he is also typically French in being afraid of the Arabs, he sees 'the blade of the knife' gleaming in the sun, reacts instinctively and kills the Arab. Maybe Camus thought just like any French man would have done in a similar situation at the time?

In the essay entitled 'Reflections on the Guillotine', Camus wrote about a case and a trial in some respects similar to the trial in *The Stranger*, 'about a French communist worker being guillotined in Africa for killing an Arab family. – The French court had to show that the guillotine was also meant for French necks.'

But Camus' main concern in this essay is his case against death penalty. Capital punishment, according to Camus, 'is obviously no less shocking than the crime itself', 'capital punishment is a disgrace to our society which its partisans cannot reasonably justify.' (Blom-Cooper 409, 412). Camus also mentions a story about his own father, vomiting after having witnessed a public execution, the same story as Meursault, imprisoned, waiting to be executed, tells about his father.

The closure of Camus' essay is noteworthy:

> Confronted with crime, how does our civilization in fact define itself? The answer is easy: for thirty years crimes of State have vastly exceeded crimes of individuals. I shall not even mention wars – general or local (...) I am referring here to the number of individuals killed directly by the State, a number that has grown to astronomic proportions and infinitely exceeds that of 'private' murders. (Blom-Cooper 444)

It is not so much against the individual killer that our society must protect itself, then, as against the State, Camus wrote, pointing to 'the blood of Algeria'.

The very last sentence in his essay goes like this: 'Neither in the hearts of men nor in the manners of society will there be a lasting peace until we have outlawed death.'

I cannot think of any better conclusion, finishing this article.

Bibliography

Blom-Cooper, Louis. *The Law as Literature*. London: Printed and bound in Great Britain for The Bodley Head Ltd 1961.

Brooks, Peter and Paul Gewirtz, eds. *Law's Stories. Narrative and Rhetoric in the Law*. New Haven: Yale University Press 1996.

Camus, Albert. *L'étranger*. Paris: Editons Gallimard 1942/1996.

Derrida, Jacques. *Politique de l'amitié*. Paris: Gallimard, 1994.

Fanon, Frantz *Les damnés de la terre*. Paris: François Maspero 1961

Johannesen, Georg. *Om den norske skrivemåten*. Oslo: Gyldendal 1981.

Linneberg, Arild. *Tolv og en halv tale om litteratur og lov og rett.* Gyldendal: Oslo 2007.
---. *Tretten triste essays om krig og litteratur.* Gyldendal: Oslo 2001.
Weisberg, Richard. *Poethics, And other Strategies of Law and Literature.* New York and Oxford: Columbia University Press 1992.
---. *The Failure of the Word.* New Haven: Yale University Press 2002.

Law as a Tale of Identity

– and Some Perspectives on Human Rights Law

Sten Schaumburg-Müller

Preliminary Confessions

When I first encountered law & literature I was both interested and sceptical. I felt interested, firstly, because I am in the hyphenated law business anyway: Legal philosophy, legal anthropology, legal sociology, law and international relations etc., so why not law and literature, and secondly, because there are some intricate legal questions as regards fiction: To what extent do individuals 'own' their own life story, how does protection of privacy and protection against defamation go together with authors' freedom of speech etc. On the other hand, I felt sceptical: Wasn't it just another hype within humanities, apparently capable of generating any kind of theory as its object is mouldable fiction rather than recalcitrant facts?

More importantly, I had an almost subconscious scepticism about authors and humanists, not because they are authors and humanists, but because they sometimes tend to think that they are more than that – or may be they do not think so themselves, but are portrayed as having a kind of privileged access to morals and truth. Authors are good at fiction – or rather good authors are good at fiction, but are they also good at facts? Or isn't it so that, say, historians are better at historical facts, political scientists better at political facts, lawyers better at legal facts, whereas authors inevitably will get some of this wrong simply because they have not studied the topics as much as the scholars. Why should authors give their opinion on EU-membership, the invasion of Iraq in 2003 or the state of the world as if they as authors have a privileged knowledge? The interviews are not presented like the weekly fashion magazine, featuring articles on how this celebrated person has furnished his or her home or on his or her relation to intimate partners etc. Apparently, the authors interviewed in relation to moral or political questions are interviewed, not because they are known, but apparently with the assumption that they, as authors, somehow know. In the same vein, humanists seem to be conceived of as simply more human than for instance lawyers who are just lawyers. My scepticism was intensified when reading an article in the Danish newspaper *Politiken* featuring an interview with law and literature representatives.

The journalist's view was obvious, though implicit: Nerdish lawyers should take in literature in order to become less juristic and more humanistic. 'Lessons in literature will improve the level' among law students, whereas literature students apparently could gain nothing from knowing anything about law, except when studying it in literature. The Danish literature professor is quoted to be 'shocked' that law students do not have a course in justice,[1] but no shock or even mentioning that literature students have no course in law, or in justice for that matter. A defence lawyer is quoted for recommending lawyers and law students to read fiction as they would gain human knowledge and insight. The journalist does not consider whether reading law such as law cases could benefit literature students (or journalists) or others, and the risk of ending up as an over-specialized nerd (as a subheading goes), is only related to law students and lawyers, not literature students or authors – or journalists for that matter.

Some months ago, a humanist scholarly journal (*Semikolon*) sent out a call for papers on human rights, and the editor invited contributions especially from 'literature, semiotics, sociology, history, philosophy and history of ideas'. The idea that the legal field could make a contribution did not even enter the humanistic mind. And the humanistic contributions to the actual issue went into sometimes interesting discussions, but at most took a superficial glance at human rights declarations, but never went into details in judgments, comments or legal literature, which often times (but not always of course) deal with highly abstract and relevant issues such as democracy, the concept of rights, universality etc.

To some extent, my scepticism is corroborated. Law and literature may be – and apparently tends to be portrayed as – literature into law rather than the opposite, humanists over lawyers rather than the merging and cooperation of two partly different scholarly fields to the benefit of both, in short culture over the technicalities of law. This makes me consider whether this way of

---

1. There is a translation problem here. There seems to be two Danish words for 'justice': 1) 'Justits' meaning the formal, rigid law connected with the state and authority, and 2) 'retfærdighed' connotes equity and a moral conception of justice. Thus the Ministry of Justice is of course 'Justitsministeriet'. The call was, of course, for a course in 'retfærdighed', the equity side of justice.

thinking is a Germanistic reminiscence of 'Kultur über Politik'. In a recent book, Wolf Lepenies has criticized the quondam German conception of being something special, *Das Land der Dichter und Denker* rather than a land of political democracy with legal rights.[2] This notion of 'culture' being above politics is, according to Lepenies, a misconception and besides it is dangerous, as the wars in the beginning of the 20th Century showed. The wars were fought under the motto: 'Am deutschen Wesen soll die Welt genesen.' One could add that if the wars in Europe on the German side were fought as culture and *Geist* against superficial market relations and democracy – with cultural defenders such as Thomas Mann (who later changed his mind) and the Norwegian Knut Hamsun (who did not) – the American side fought in favour of market economy, political democracy and, in this connection importantly, legal rights.

I am of course not trying to side the humanistic approach with the Nazi-German atrocities, but I am trying to criticize the 'culture above politics and law'-attitude that seems to have German roots and is as inappropriate in war as well as in law and literature, and I am trying to make the point that law and the engagement in legal matters is no less important, no less moral and no less human than engaging in literature etc. To think otherwise is a 'cultural obsession'.

Admittedly, law and especially legal philosophy such as the Scandinavian realism has contributed to the notion that lawyers are merely technicians, strictly detached from values and political ideas. However, this special branch of legal philosophy has been abandoned back in the 1970's, at least by legal philosophers, whereas lawyers trained from the mid 1940's to the mid 1970's still may hold this conception as their more or less subconscious notion of law, as a kind of tacit concept of law. And the general public, including journalists, may also still be of the conception that law is formal technique and lawyers are technical nerds.

In order for law and literature to make sense, I contend that law and literature should be on equal footing and not a mission of bringing culture into culture lacking law. Law and literature are two different scholarly fields which by way of 'law and literature' could (re)discover some of their common ground. The remainder of this contribution is but one attempt and one possible approach to do so.

---

2. Wolf Lepenies, *Kultur und Politik. Deutsche Geschichten.*; in an apparently abridged translation: *The Seduction of Culture in German History.*

Law as a Tale of Identity

There are many possible – and probably even more impossible – ways of conceiving law. According to the American realist Karl Llewelyn, law is what officials do about disputes, according to the British positivist John Austin law is orders backed by threat, and according to Herbert Hart law is the union of primary and secondary rules. These – and many more – may have grasped a part of what law is, an aspect, a view of law. My contention here is that law can equally be conceived as a tale of identity, as a narrative of who we are. Maybe this aspect does not work for all types of law, but I think it works for some.

When our kids were small we introduced a rule saying: No singing at the dinner table. This was, as the kids grew up, later interpreted into including: No drumming at the table, including no use of knives and forks as drumsticks and plates and glasses as drums. In retrospect I realize that this rule was probably more identity creating than norm setting. By asking the children, they confirm that there was not more singing going on at dinner tables in their friends' houses (or drumming for that matter), even though the other families did not have any rule regarding such activities. The rule, then, was not so much a question of dispute resolution or orders backed by threat, even though it was a primary rule (secondary rules being as absent in our family as in Hart's conception of primitive societies). Rather, it was a small tale of identity: This is who we are, exactly like other families were telling their tales of identity by having rules like prohibiting champing the food noisily – without this resulting in conspicuously more or less noise, but rather in a (slightly) different identity: They are the ones who do not like champing the food in contradiction to others who, like us, restricted individual singing at the table.

Leviticus (23:18) lays down a prohibition from having sex with animals. Whether the Israelites actually had more or less sex with animals than their surrounding neighbors, we do not know, but I doubt that there was much difference. Rather, the provisions serve as identity markers: 'You must not do as they do in Egypt, where you used to live, and you must not do as they do in the land of Canaan, where I am bringing you' (Leviticus 23:3), a rather obvious indication that this is a question of identity.

The point here is that we are not only what we are or what we do, but also who we think we are, who we want to be, who we present us to be and who we think we ought to be. And law and norms are part of that presentation.

When a new government was formed in Denmark in 2002, the Minister of Justice put forward a proposal in Parliament of longer prison terms for perpetrators of violence. She stated that longer prison terms may not have any influence on the crime rate, but she wanted the bill carried through because of its symbolic value. This approach can also be seen as an identity maker: This is who we are, the present Conservative-Liberal government, and we do not like violence, in (alleged) contradiction to the previous Social Democratic-Social Liberal government. Even the legislators do not merely conceive legislation as a means of bringing about certain effects, but in this case rather as a means of identity.

Of course, not only law is creating identity, but also other norms may be involved, such as norms of not abiding by the law. However, law can be seen as a narrative of identity, a tale concerning important life questions, including questions of identity.

This law as a narrative of identity-approach may shed some light on the present human rights situation and debate in Denmark.

Two Versions of the Same Story

As regards substantive law, there is little difference between Danish and European human rights protection. Denmark was a whole-hearted supporter of the European Convention on Human Rights (ECHR), and the official policy has quite consistently been a human rights supporting one, at home as well as abroad, even though the term 'human rights' has not always been used. Denmark has a very low score of convictions before the European Human Rights Court (hereafter simply the Court): 29 judgments of which 6 ended up with the Court finding Denmark in breach of its human rights obligations. In comparison, Austria has had 232 judgment and Italy 1811 with a population size 1½ and 10 times bigger than Denmark, respectively.[3]

As of late criticism has been voiced. I am not focusing on the human rights opponents, quite strong in the Danish People's Party, a supporter of the present Danish government. Rather, I am focusing on human rights proponents who are somewhat sceptical towards the seemingly ever increasing human rights protection from the Council of Europe and especially the Court.

Part of the explanation of this scepticism, I believe, can be found in the different ways of depicting human rights, the differing tales of identity. When Danish lawyers encounter the European human rights system, they may get

---

3. Case figures from the official website of the Council of Europe. I have not counted up the number of convictions for Austria or Italy. Denmark was found in breach of its obligations in the following cases: Hauschildt, Jersild, A & Others, Vasileva, Rasmussen & Sørensen and Iversen.

into some kind of identity problem: Hey, this is not the way we are, this is not how the story goes.

The European tale has left almost all canonized European political philosophy behind: Where Hobbes favored the absolute sovereign and disregarded individual rights, the Court, of course, favours individual rights and rejects the idea of an absolute sovereign. Rousseau favoured democracy, but did not care much for individual rights, and his idea of separation of powers only related to the executive and the legislature as he was not concerned with courts. The Court, in contradiction, cares much for individual rights, the independence of courts and a well-functioning democracy. More surprisingly perhaps, the Court differs from the father of rights, John Locke, by rejecting the notion of pre-set rights and instead insisting on contextual rights, adjustable to present day conditions. Besides, Locke was no ardent proponent of democracy, but rather saw a limited representative government as the best way to protect the natural rights. The Court, in contradiction, sees democracy as a value in itself and takes great effort to find ways of solving the often difficult questions relating to the relationship between individual rights on the one hand and democracy and the common interest on the other.

Even Montesquieu is left out of the tale with his insistence on the tripartition of powers and his idea of the courts as 'the mouth of the law'. The Court is not particularly concerned with the tripartition, but has its main focus on the independence of the judiciary, which in addition is no mere mouth, but an active law generating agent participating in securing individual rights and securing legal room for and protection of democracy.

In a way, the Court is telling quite a new version of the human rights story in which we find no eternal truths, no holy founding fathers and no sovereigns. Instead we find an active storyteller, not merely reiterating the same old story, but adding to it, and perpetually trying to balance the interests of the individual and the interests of the community without any hero designated in advance.

As any other story, the European human rights tale may not always be convincing, the Vasileva case being but one example.[4] But the most problem-

4. Vasileva was a free rider on buses of my home town. When asked to produce a travel document, she refused, and she refused to convey her name and address. The police arrived, and she still refused, this now being a minor criminal offense. In Denmark, we do not have identity cards, but individuals are required to indicate their name and address when asked to do so by the police. Upon refusing, she was taken into custody which lasted from 9.30 at night until 11.00 in the morning, by which time she revealed her identity. The Court found the duration of the detention unproportionate.

atic feature of the story is probably its lack of limitation: Anything can be included into the story of human rights, which then runs the risk of losing the ability to hold the attention of the audience, and as a consequence, thereby losing its potential as an identity maker.

The Danish story of human rights is different. It may not even conceive itself as a story of human rights, but rather as a story of a relatively small community being relatively successful in creating law, progress and welfare for its members.

The Danish story still includes important parts of the European political philosophical canon: Hobbes' idea of a sovereign creating the necessary commonwealth for its subjects is still prevailing, although, of course, the sovereign has now turned into a benevolent one, a voluntary shift for the sake of its own survival and the welfare of its subjects. Rousseau, who kept the idea of an absolute sovereign, but switched the subject from a king into the people, is also included in the Danish story of a democratic community aiming at the general interest, and Montesquieu has his place in the opening section of the Constitution with the tripartition of powers, although the legislation in the Danish version is jointly made up by a Parliament and the King, i.e. the executive. The courts are somehow conceived as the mouth of the law and not really supposed to mingle with politics or create law which would amount to an intrusion in democracy.

The Danish story is much more about law than about rights, and law is a matter of policy which is located in the national Parliament, the Folketing, and to some extent in the local municipalities (the Danish term being 'kommune', implying the common). 'Nothing above and nothing beside the Folketing', was a catchword in the late 19th century, and it is still a part of the tale. Presently, journalists are mainly of the opinion that important political questions ought to be solved at 'Christiansborg', (Parliament & government), not at irrelevant places like the EU, the national courts or the Council of Europe etc. (Lund 215)

When the Danish People's Party proposed to criminalize the burning of Dannebrog, the Danish flag, the proposal was turned down in the Parliament, not with reference to human rights, limiting the Parliament's powers to reduce freedom of speech, but with reference to the political tradition: We are liberals, we do not like burnings of the flag, but we do not criminalize people even if we don't like them. Human rights protection is definitely not absent in Denmark, but it is not a tradition of rights, but rather a tradition of political goodwill. It is la volonté générale, the general interest to protect individual freedoms. Individuals do not have these rights as a matter of nature or because the European Human Rights Court says so, but because this is the will of the people.

Thus, the version of the story is quite different, but the content as relating to the protection of human rights is quite similar, with a few discrepancies.

Freedom of Speech as Example

The Danish Constitution has a freedom of speech clause which except for a minor addition has remained unaltered since 1849: 'Any person shall be at liberty to publish his ideas in print, in writing, or in speech, subject to his being held responsible before a court of law,' basically a 'freedom of speech within the law'-model as art. 11 of the French Declaration of Human and Citizens' Rights. In addition, censorship was never again to be introduced. In 1849, censorship was in focus as the much despised practice of absolutism, whereas the balance between constitutional protection vis-à-vis restrictive legislation was not clear.

There seems to be no court practice from the first decennia following constitutional rule, and the doctrinal conception seems to be one of freedom of speech as the point of departure with restrictions as the necessary exception. However, in the late 19th Century the first doctrinal attack was launched. The conservative legal scholar, member of the Upper House and representative of the minority government party, Carl Goos, held that the Constitution would never protect unlawful expressions, and – pop! – any constitutional protection against legislative or even administrative restrictions became impossible. By this time, the government, appointed by the King, had no parliamentary backing and therefore issued 'administrative legislation', including prohibition of criticism of the government, a practice accepted by the courts.

The second attack was launched in the mid-20th Century by the legal scholar Alf Ross, who even though he was not a member of Parliament, was a strong and outspoken supporter of the Social Democratic government then in power. He was an ardent defender of freedom of speech as a wise policy, but dismissed as ardently any constitutional protection. According to his view, the legislator had the power to make any restriction as regards restriction of freedom of speech, as long as it did not amount to censorship. But, of course, the legislature had better use this power wisely – as a matter of policy, that is, not as a matter of respect for existing individual rights.

In accordance with this idea of unlimited freedom of the Parliament and the government rather than individual freedom of speech, the courts never referred to the Constitution in freedom of speech cases. In 1937 the then Minister of Justice initiated a defamation suit against a political opponent who had used quite abusive words. Except for one charge (of treason) the case was dismissed, not with reference to the Constitution nor to any individual right, but to the prevailing political debate. The court would not interfere with the rather harsh verbal political climate, thus in fact using 'politicians' custom' rather than the Constitution as the relevant legal source.

As the Parliament never introduced bills restricting freedom of speech highly out of proportion, the freedom of speech state of affairs was by and large good and acceptable, with – however – a somewhat conformal touch: Criticism 'upwards' (against politicians and leaders) tended to be treated more severely by the courts than criticism 'downwards' (criticism by politicians and leaders). Besides, after the Second World War, any use of 'racist', 'anti-Semite' and 'Nazi' opinions would be penalized if brought before the courts, this being, I believe, part of the Danish narration of identity: We are not racists or anti-Semites in contradistinction to the former Nazi-Germany. We are Danes, not Germans, and definitely not Nazis.

The European human rights protection of freedom of speech can be summarized as follows:

- Freedom of speech is the rule, restrictions the exception;
- Expressions relating to issues of genuine public interest are highly protected and restrictions almost unimaginable;
- Expressions (and pictures) relating to the genuine private sphere are equally highly protected;
- Politicians enjoy a wide freedom of speech and in return must accept severe criticism (that is: both 'up-' and 'downwards' critique is protected);
- Journalists etc. have a wide freedom of speech, especially when passing on the expressions of others. In return they must live up to basic requirements of ethics of journalism, such as checking their sources, giving room for counter-opinions etc.;
- As long as expressions have some factual basis, even quite abusive words will be qualified as value judgments, protected by the freedom of speech;
- Issues relating to morals (mainly sex), religion and commerce are to a large extent left to the national jurisdictions.

Hopefully the reader can trace certain differences in the protection of freedom of speech between the European human rights tradition and the Danish.

However, around the mid 1970's – the time when the European Court of Human Rights really started to take off – one can observe a change in the

Danish perception. The Danish courts started referring, not to rights, let alone constitutional rights, but to the principle of issues of public interests, acquitting persons charged with defamation who according to a strict reading of the Penal Code, ought to be convicted. At least one clear cut example of a wider freedom for journalists can be traced to 1980, a year in which the 'expressor' of racist remarks was convicted, whereas the editor who published them was acquitted, and even before that time the journalists had a certain 'privilege of reference', together with lawyers and defence attorneys.

The change in Danish law was not geared by the European Court or European human rights, which were only taken in as relevant legal sources starting around 1990. As I see it, the trends were simultaneous, but independent, and, interestingly, going in the same direction. From 1990 onwards it is hardly possible to distinguish a specific Danish and a specific European tradition in relation to freedom of speech, as Danish law started to include European human rights law.

Thus, even with the partly differing traditions, it is still possible to speak of two stories with almost the same content, but told in quite different ways.

Are Legal Narratives Important?

Probably the two versions of the human rights tale are more important for lawyers who in their daily professional life are reiterating the Danish legal narrative. Others are more likely to have different tales of identity, simply not knowing what Danish law is about anyway. To equate a national legal culture with the national culture is, of course, not well-founded.

On the other hand also politicians are telling the tale of who we are, and they are doing so in terms of law, simply because they are part of the legislature. To a large extent they participate in reiterating the story of a small country who knows how to solve its problems, which is not done by means of prefixed or externally decided individual rights, but by internal political deliberations. And, as noted, journalists tend to think that any problem appearing in Denmark should be solved by Danish politicians, not by courts, lawyers or international tribunals. And there we have it: The tale of identity is told to the public at large on a daily basis.

Therefore, I believe, the legal narrative is also important. Returning to the opening issue, in the interview Wolf Lepenies quoted a German filmmaker for announcing that only culture can give Europe a soul. But not only filmmakers are telling stories and not only culture can create common ground.

Law, politics and economics are equally important storytellers, and their say is at least as important as that of culture.

Bibliography

Bech-Danielsen, Anne. 'Kafka, Camus – og Karnov.' Politiken 5 July 2007.

Jensen, Jesper Wind. 'Den kulturelle besættelse'. Weekendavisen 13 July 2007: 10-11.

Lepenies, Wolf. *Kultur und Politik. Deutsche Geschichten.* Carl Hanser Verlag 2006.

Lepenies, Wolf. *The Seduction of Culture in German History.* Princeton University Press 2006.

Lund, Anker Brink. *Den redigerende magt. Nyhedsinstitutionens politiske indflydelse,* [The editing power. The political influence of media]. Århus: Århus Universitetsforlag 2002.

Europe as Contested Terrain:

On European Narratives of Human Rights

Helle Porsdam

In a call for papers for the 'Women in German Annual Conference 2007,' the organizers introduce the notion of Europe as 'contested terrain':

> The transatlantic tensions in the run-up to the Iraq invasion produced, for a while, the heady possibilities of imagining Europe as counter-weight to American-style globalization. And while some believe that that utopian window has closed, we think it is still necessary to explore Europe as contested terrain – caught between colonial, imperialist, fascist, and totalitarian histories and their legacies (Pim Fortuyn's Europe, as Arjun Appadurai has called it), and the enlightened, post-Eurocentric, antifascist Europe that is committed to learning its lessons from the past (Bassam Tibi's Europe) ('Contesting Europe: Feminist Critiques and Globalization').

In this paper, I, too, wish to explore Europe as contested terrain. My main argument will be that Europeans have attempted for some time to develop their own version of what Mary Ann Glendon once called, in the American context, 'rights talk': A human rights talk. European intellectuals as well as European Union politicians and policy professionals are talking about the need to construct 'European narratives.' What they have in mind are narratives that will emphasize a political, but also a cultural, vision for a multiethnic and more cosmopolitan Europe. These narratives evolve around human rights, partly because their authors hope that they may function as a kind of cultural glue in an increasingly multiethnic Europe, and partly because they are intimately connected with that part of Enlightenment thinking that sought to promote democracy and the rule of law.

In addition, modern Europe is 'self-reflexive,' argues German sociologist Ulrich Beck; it is built on a conscious wish to learn from the terrible mistakes of the past, and this also makes human rights central. Human rights, that is, are developing into a discourse of atonement as well as of hope for these

Europeans. It is a discourse that speaks to Bassam Tibi's, and not Pim Fontuyn's, Europe – to the enlightened, post-Eurocentric, antifascist Europe that is committed to learning its lessons from the past.

My paper will be divided into two parts. I will start by discussing why it is that there currently seems to be a need in Europe for constructing European narratives. In the second part, I will look at current European literature and briefly offer three examples of European narratives of human rights.

I. Why the need to construct European narratives?

In 2005, in national referenda, first the French and then the Dutch voted against the proposed European Constitutional Treaty. And in 2008, the Irish voted 'no' to its successor, the Lisbon Treaty. This put on display – for the whole world to see – the skepticism with which the peoples of Europe still view the idea of forming an ever-stronger political union. That it was issues of a domestic nature that ultimately made people vote the way they did, furthermore made it quite clear how marred European politics have been over the years by the pursuit of narrow, national interests. When we add to this the expansion of the EU towards the east and the ever-present question of Turkey's possibly joining the EU, we have, I think, one part of the answer as to why the need for the construction of a European consciousness or identity arose during the past few years. The steady immigration, legal as well as illegal, from Muslim and African countries has furthermore made identity politics – and the need to formulate a set of common rules – more noticeable and pressing.

A human rights framework, moreover, is by and large a secular one. It is not secular in the sense that it seeks to prevent people from being or becoming religious, freedom of religion being one of the most important of political and cultural rights, after all. It is secular, rather, in the sense that it encourages the separation of church and state and wants to turn religion into a private matter. With religion presently (re)surfacing in Europe as an important, but highly divisive cultural factor, it has become important for some European intellectuals and policy makers to insist on a secular human rights framework for Europe. The discussion about whether or not the Christian tradition ought to be mentioned in the Preamble to the European Constitutional Treaty was a good example of this. A born-again Christian president in the USA (George W. Bush) between 2000 and 2008 and the insistence on a religious view of the world in many other parts of the world may give us one more part of the answer as to why European narratives of human rights are presently being constructed.

But there is something else going on, too, as I hope to show. There is a feeling of recovery that is beginning to make itself felt. Europe may slowly be healing, and this brings with it a feeling of hope for the future. Europe is like a patient in therapy for whom there is hope when she is finally able to put into words what has happened to her, and how she feels about it. Nothing can ever make undone the terrible deeds of the past, and Europeans will always be burdened with the guilt that goes with their past. And indeed, if they should forget they would soon be reminded and be brought to their senses by non-Europeans. Intellectual currents or movements such as post-modernity and post-colonialism have done exactly that: They have reminded Europeans of the effects on others of their arrogant behavior in the past and thereby humbled any European attempt to suggest that European values are unique and absolute.

For European intellectuals such as Ulrich Beck and Bassam Tibi – just to mention a couple of scholars whose work touches upon issues concerning European identity – the time has come to move on. Born in Damaskus and raised in the Middle-East before coming to Germany to study with members of the Frankfurt school, Tibi later became a professor of international relations at the University of Göttingen and the author of several books on modern Arab history and politics. He argues that Europeans have been too slow to acknowledge the need for a 'Leitkultur' ('leading culture'), a set of common rules for the behavior of Europeans, new as well as old. In their eagerness not to appear intolerant and bigoted, Europeans have lost touch with the best part of Enlightenment thinking: Respect for individual rights and freedoms. As a result,

> Europeans [now] seem to need a second Enlightenment, an inter-cultural dialogue during which they decide on their relationship with the rest of the non-European world. As part of the assignment, they need to de-romanticize their ethnically exclusive way of thinking. However, this should not lead to a false sense of self-denial ... As the core of the European cultural modern, they need to insist on a catalogue of norms and values for others as well as for themselves. I call such a catalogue a 'Leitkultur' (Bassam Tibi 183).[1]

1. My translation from the German ('Die Europäer scheinen einer zweiten Aufklärung zu bedürfen, in deren Rahmen sie ihr Verhältnis zum nicht-europäischen Rest der Welt im inter-kulturellen Dialog bestimmen. Zu den Aufgaben gehört, ihr ethnisch-exklusives

Helle Porsdam

Tibi sees Islamic fundamentalism as a modern totalitarian political movement that misuses popular religious devotion. In the global fragmentation that has emerged from the end of the Cold War, such Islamic fundamentalism threatens to provoke a new world disorder. Brought up in the Islamic faith himself, Tibi has nothing against Islamic spiritual faith. It is Islamic fundamentalism, which he sees as a primarily political and deeply problematic response to Western dominance. The fundamentalist revolt, he explains, targets not just Western political power but Western culture and value as well – hence the need for a 'Leitkultur.'[2]

German sociologist Ulrich Beck, too, believes in a 'Leitkultur' of sorts.[3] He calls his vision of the new Europe a 'cosmopolitan Europe.' It is a Europe which has admitted to and worked through the many mistakes of the past – a self-reflexive Europe. And it is a Europe which has come to see that there are elements of European intellectual thinking that are worth preserving. Again, these evolve around individual rights and cultural diversity.

In *Das kosmopolitische Europa* (Cosmopolitan Europe), published in 2004, the point of departure for Beck and his co-author Edgar Grande is that

Denkens zu entromantisieren. Allerdings dürfen sie damit nicht fälschlich eine Selbstverleugnung verbinden ... Auf dem Boden der europäischen kulturellen Moderne müssen sie einen Normen- und Werte-Katalog verbindlich für sich und andere verlangen. Ich nenne diesen Katalog Leitkultur.') – Several of Tibi's books have been translated into English.

2. The term, '*Leitkultur*,' created quite a stir when it was first introduced. For European intellectuals, it had unfortunate echoes of a Europe that used to consider itself better, more refined than everybody else. Furthermore, it suggested that 'culture' can be talked about in the singular – something that is deeply problematic for intellectuals who value diversity and pluralism. For a while, the very term effectively blocked for a discussion of Tibi's arguments, and he could probably have saved himself a lot of trouble by choosing a different one. The term was, Tibi claims, misused during the German general election of 2005 and thus ended up having mostly negative connotations – connotations that were never intended on his part. What he did intend the word to connote, he writes in the introduction to *Europa ohne Identität* is 'nothing else but an orientation, a kind of red thread in the form of a value consensus concerning civilizational European values such as secular democracy, individual (*not* collective) human rights, civil society, tolerance as well as religious and cultural pluralism' – my translation from the German ('Dabei meint der Begriff 'Leitkultur' ... nichts anderes als eine Orientierung, eine Art Leitfaden in Form eines Wertekonsenses über zivilisatorische europäische Werte wie sakuläre Demokratie, individuelle (*nicht* kollektive) Menschenrechte, Zivilgesellschaft, Toleranz sowie religiösen und kulturellen Pluralismus.')

3. The following pages concerning the work of Ulrich Bech and Edgar Grande, and the 'Official EU European Narratives' are taken from my article, 'On European Narratives of Human Rights and Their Possible Implications for Copyright,'

82

'Europe has to be thought anew.'(*Das kosmopolitische Europa* 7).[4] Europe is presently going through a crisis. Not only did the attempt to make the peoples of Europe approve of a common Constitutional Treaty fail; European member states also keep pursuing their own, narrow nation-state agendas and have utterly failed to integrate all the new immigrants coming to their countries. Institutional reforms will no longer do the trick; they cannot create the feeling of belonging and solidarity that is needed for Europeans to take a more positive attitude toward the European project. What might help foster such a sense of solidarity, however, is a 'European narrative.' It is a narrative that has to be constructed – 'Europe cannot be found, it must be invented.'(Beck and Grande, *Das kosmopolitische Europa* 18).[5]

The new European narrative is a supra-national or 'cosmopolitan narrative.' At its core is a combination of two things: A positive view of multiethnic diversity and a wish to work towards a form of political democracy which no longer revolves around the nation-state. The European project and its narrative is also a 'reflexive' one. Europeans are currently, Beck and Grande argue, in 'the second' and 'reflexive modern'. The nation-state was the basis of 'the first modern', but at the moment Europeans are being forced into new and more international relations with others. They experience different actors at work in society than nation-states – actors like for example networks, experts and NGOs. Europe is both a product of and a driving force behind this whole process. In a post-colonial acknowledgement of all that was negative in European history, Europeans have self-critically or reflexively made the choice to break away from their militant past.

As Beck and Grande see it, modern Europe has developed out of a conscious attempt to come to terms with and never forget the past. In this, the realization of the importance of self-criticism, Beck and Grande hint, Europe may well be different from both the United States and Islamic societies: 'Is it perhaps this radical, self-critical confrontation with its own history that makes Europe different from, for example, the United States or the Islamic socie-

4. 'Europa muss neu gedacht werden.' – I thank translator and scholar Manuela Thurner who has translated this and the following passages from Beck and Grande from the German. The book is the last in a trilogy of books which marks an attempt on Beck's part to develop a 'cosmopolitan realism.' The first two books are *Macht und Gegenmacht im globalen Zeitalter* and *Der kosmopolitische Blick*.
5. 'Europa kann nicht *ge*funden werden, es muss *er*funden werden.'

ties?' (Beck and Grande, *Das kosmopolitische Europa* 21).[6] If there is much *not* to be proud of, this is one kind of 'European exceptionalism' that Europeans *can* be proud of, they suggest.

Human rights form a very important component of Beck's and Grande's vision for a better Europe. Indeed, it could hardly be otherwise, their vision resulting from a self-critical reflection on the crimes of European history. It was during the Nuremberg trials that the world first heard of 'crimes against humanity', the Nuremberg court being the first truly international court to prosecute such crimes and the first to create international categories of law that went beyond the sovereignty of the nation-state.

The transnationalization of human rights in opposition to the legal sovereignty of the individual nation-states is thus the key, for Beck and Grande, to the creation of a European civil society. The universal or cosmopolitan quality of human rights serves a further purpose, too. Human rights guarantee diversity, but they also form a set of common rules according to which that very diversity can be regulated and integrated. This point about a cosmopolitan Europe being both one of difference/diversity *and* integration is an important one for Beck and Grande.

Europe must be 'done' – must be lived on a day-to-day basis by the peoples of Europe. At best, 'doing Europe' will be a grass-roots endeavor. While we are waiting for this to happen, certain supra-national European institutions are doing their best to make the dream of cosmopolitan Europe come true. Chief among these, argue Beck and Grande, is the European Court of Justice (ECJ). Much like the U.S. Supreme Court, the ECJ has created a supranational law that trumps that of the individual states. It has thus become a 'cosmopolitan entrepreneur who, by virtue of the law, succeeds in gaining some ground for a cosmopolitan Europe against a nationalist Europe.' (Beck and Grande, *Das kosmopolitische Europa* 19)[7]

Like most other Europeans who set out to discuss Europe and the European project, Beck and Grande contrast and compare it to the United States. The transatlantic relationship forms an important subtext throughout, and while the two authors are careful to emphasize the importance of cooperating with the USA, they cannot quite hide their wish to promote Europe

6. 'Ist es vielleicht diese radikale selbstkritische Konfrontation mit der eigener Geschichte, die Europa beispielsweise von den USA oder den islamischen Gesellschaften unterscheidet?'
7. 'Kosmopolitischen Unternehmer, der mit der Macht des Rechts ein Stück kosmopolitisches Europa gegen das nationale Europa durchsetzt.'

as an alternative to the USA Characteristically, the very last words of the book concern the transatlantic relationship:

> Then there will be, all over the world, an alternative to the *American way*, a *European way* which will focus on the rule of law, political equality, social justice, cosmopolitan integration and solidarity. (Beck and Grande, *Das kosmopolitische Europa* 393)[8]

Official European Union narratives

We see these arguments and analyses reflected in the attempts made over the past decade or so by the EU and its policy professionals to find in the area of culture and cultural politics answers to some of Europe's most pressing problems. Realizing that neither economic nor political visions of a united Europe have been able to create a sense of common identity among the peoples of Europe, EU policy professionals have turned to 'culture' as a possible instrument for popularizing Europe.

Until 1992, when the Maastricht Treaty on European Union brought the area of culture within the jurisdiction of the Community, purely economic reasons were used for achieving cultural ends. The cultural goals of the Community now came to be outlined in Title IX, Article 128 of the Maastricht Treaty (later to become Article 151 of the Treaty of Amsterdam): 'The Community shall contribute to the flowering of the cultures of the Member States, while respecting their national and regional diversity and at the same time bringing the common cultural heritage to the fore.' It ends by demanding that 'the Community shall take cultural aspects into account in its actions under other provisions of this Treaty' – thus assigning to 'culture' a very high priority.

The official EU European narrative, moreover, is very much a human rights narrative. 'The formation of Europe – and of the European Communities and the Union that lie at the heart of the continent's political life – has largely been expressed in legal terms,' as Philip Ruttley puts it. On 'the long road' towards European unity and integration, the law has made a large contribution. (Ruttley 228) It was the Treaty of Amsterdam of 1997 amending the Maastricht Treaty from 1992 that truly made explicit the human rights foundation of the Union: New applicant states must honor and observe the

---

8. 'Dann gibt es welt-weit eine Alternative zum *American way*, einen *European way*, der die Herrschaft des Rechts, politische Gleichheit, soziale Gerechtigkeit, kosmopolitische Integration und Solidarität ins Zentrum stellt.'

rights outlined in the European Convention of HR; if they do not, they become liable to legal action.

In a 2007 publication by the European Commission, 'The European Union: Furthering Human Rights and Democracy Across the Globe,' it is stated in the Introduction that, 'liberty, democracy, respect for human rights and fundamental freedoms, and the rule of law, are founding principles of the European Union and an indispensable prerequisite for the Union's legitimacy.' A bit further on, the importance of 'mainstreaming human rights and democratization' is explained: 'Mainstreaming is the process of integrating human rights and democratization issues into all aspects of EU policy decision-making and implementation, including external assistance. European institutions are deeply committed to intensify the mainstreaming of human rights.'

II. 'Europe writes': Law and literature, European-style

The movement known as 'law and literature' started in the mid-1980s in the United States. Scholars who 'do' law and literature are concerned with the possible meeting-points of the two disciplines law and literature – one such meeting-point being hermeneutics (the interpretation of texts), another rhetoric. It was mostly lawyers/law professors who were initially interested in this new discipline, and there was much talk of how to make legal education better and more suitable to a totally legalized society such as the American – the point being made that perhaps if law students studied works of literature, they would learn something useful about empathy, about how laws and decisions made by people in power affect other people.

In Europe, too, law and literature is slowly becoming a field of interest to people in the humanities. There are a number of similarities between the American and European 'branches' of law and literature. The most obvious one is the use of a rights discourse. European societies are becoming more rights-oriented and more oriented towards constitutional democracy with judicial review and a stronger role to play for the courts, which is reflected in European discourse and cultural life. As I have argued elsewhere, I see this, at least in part, as an Americanization.[9] It is when we consider the contents of

---

9. See e.g. *From civil to human rights: Dialogues on law and humanities in the United States and Europe* in which many of the arguments presented here are dealt with in more depth.

the two dialects – what is actually said and argued – that the differences start emerging.

The main differences between European human rights talk and American rights talk concern first of all the *kinds* of (human) rights emphasized, and secondly the attitude towards international law and international human rights regimes. Whereas Americans tend to be mostly interested in first-generation human rights (civil and political rights), Europeans are, generally speaking, more willing also to consider second- and third-generation rights (economic, social, and cultural rights). As an American colleague once put it to me: 'In Europe, you have human rights – in the USA, we have civil rights.'

Europeans increasingly talk about the 'indivisibility' of human rights and do not agree with American arguments that the core of human rights is made up of first-generation rights only. When it comes to the international situation, Europeans are, again generally speaking, more willing to promote international law and human rights institutions than are Americans – even at the 'cost' of subsuming national law and national concerns under those of supra-national law.

These differences notwithstanding, I am of the opinion that American rights talk and European human rights talk are *dialects* of the same rights discourse rather than two fundamentally different discourses. In the USA, rights dominate the notion of citizenship from the top to the bottom of the system. This is not quite – or not yet – the case in Europe where the dialect of rights and responsibilities associated with the Romano-Germanic legal traditions makes for a somewhat more nuanced dialect.

Since the fall of the Berlin wall in 1989, European artists have started discussing Europe and a possible European identity in their works. This is happening very slowly – and sometimes without great enthusiasm – but it is happening. In this literature as in the more official European narratives, there are various versions of the European project at play. Some writers allow themselves to hope that the welfare state may survive at the supra-national level. Others have European dreams of a multiethnic and tolerant Europe or see in a strong Europe the possibility of either a feminist or an environmentally sounder space. And for still others, 'Europe' signifies a consumer paradise in which you can buy your way to happiness. Utopian – but also their opposite, dystopian – 'Europes' are definitely finding their way into cultural, artistic and political discussions these days.

There do seem to be a couple of things, though, that many of these European writers share. As already touched upon, the notion of rights is broader in the European context than in the American. It has to do with human dignity, generally speaking, and with equality – social and cultural just as much as political. This is where the emphasis on economic, social and cultural rights comes in, human dignity presupposing for many European writers an access to welfare rights in one form or another.

In addition, these European writers insist on their right to be critical and to ask questions. In its representation of life as uncomplicated and sunny, popular culture – especially, but not exclusively, that originating in the USA – offers a surface treatment only of issues that deserve much more careful treatment. Again, it is the self-reflexive quality of a Europe that has lost its naiveté and its feeling of superiority which is pointed out by those writers. As far as they are concerned, a Europe that reflects, remembers, and hesitates, before it acts, is to be preferred to a USA that considers fast response to world matters a virtue in and of itself.

Three examples of European human rights narratives
Let me offer, finally, some more concrete examples of European human rights narratives. Many others could be mentioned, but these are the ones that I am currently interested in.

a. Europe as a feminist narrative:
Conscious that the 'Founding Fathers' of the EU were all male, the European Commission, the European Parliament and the European Movement instituted a new prize in 1987: The Women of Europe Award. The plan was to correct this male bias by giving official recognition to women who had made outstanding contributions to 'European construction.' According to many feminists, a recognition of the contribution of Europe's women was long overdue. It came at an important time, too. For many years, most talk in the European context of 'equality' referred to the equality between the sexes. With much more focus in the 1980s and 90s on ethnic diversity, however, 'equality' increasingly came to be associated with racial and ethnic equality. This coincided with the end or demise of the first modern wave of feminism which had been related to the various youth movements of the 1960s.

The 1990s saw the birth of a new awareness of women's issues, as these related both to the daughters of the first modern feminist 'generation' and to the women of ethnic minorities in Europe. One of the venues for this renewed interest in feminist issues, interestingly enough, was the detective novel. In the USA, female detective writers such as Sara Paretsky and Sue Grafton had used the detective novel as a forum in which to discuss issues of importance to women already in the late 1970s and early 80s. Now, ten to fifteen years later, that idea was taken up by their European sisters. Only, the concerns of Scandinavian writers such as Norwegian writer Anna Holt, Swedish writer

88

Lisa Marklund and Danish writer Elsebeth Egholm were and are somewhat different. Whereas Paretsky's novels focus on the personal development of her main character V.I. Warshawski, for example, the Scandinavian heroines are typically very concerned with the relationship and obligation of the individual towards her friends, family, and society in general. For the latter, moreover, it is gender as it is structured and created by society more than it is constructed by the individual woman that is at the center of attention.

The language used by the Scandinavian feminist detective writers is not necessarily a rights language, but they use a genre that has always been associated with law and lawyers – the detective novel – to focus on issues of female dignity and identity, more broadly speaking.

b. European narratives of consumption:
Women have often been associated with consumption. From the beginning of the 20th century when advertisement started to become big business, advertisers have targeted women because they perceived them to be especially susceptible to the lures of consumption. While not a major issue in the Scandinavian feminist detective novels discussed above, consumption figured as feminine does surface from time to time. It becomes more tangible in another context, though, and that is in some of the recent writings about (Western) Europe by Eastern European writers. In *Café Europa: Life after communism*, published in 1996, Slavenka Drakulic movingly describes the yearning of Eastern Europeans for the consumer goods so amply available in Western Europe. In her particular case, the gender issue becomes more acute, because she is married to a Western European (a Swede) who does not understand her sense of obligation towards friends staying behind in Eastern Europe. She has herself moved to Vienna, and every time she goes back to Eastern Europe she takes all kinds of consumer goods with her to please her old friends.

Gender is linked for Drakulic to consumption in another, and much more dramatic way as well. In a later book, *S: A Novel About the Balkans* (2001), she tells the story of the systematic mass rape, sexual enslavement and torture of Bosnian women and girls between 1992 and '95. The place where this physical abuse took place, we are told, was a 'storehouse of women,' a place where female bodies were stored for the use of men. For the Serbian soldiers and paramilitaries who did this, women were reduced to objects that they could consume at will.

In an article in *The Nation*, Drakulic relates her novel to a collection of some forty accounts by Muslim women who were raped in 1992. *I Begged Them to Kill Me*, as this collection was called, was sent and dedicated to Drakulic because she herself had been brave enough to talk about the sexual crimes that would later be defined as crimes against humanity. The decision of the Muslim women to spread the information about what had happened to them later led to some of them testifying before the International Criminal Tribunal for Yugoslavia in The Hague. From our perspective it is interesting to note the belief on the part of these women that justice might indeed be done through this Tribunal and its human rights discourse. Drakulic writes:

> Women who were raped before them, in Germany, China and Korea during the two world wars, rarely spoke about it in public. It was not to be mentioned but to be forgotten. Indeed, it was forgotten. However, the raped women in Bosnia believed in the possibility of justice through the International Criminal Tribunal for Yugoslavia in The Hague, established by the UN Security Council in 1993. And they understood that justice could not be done without their help. In the book, all of the violated women say they would volunteer as witnesses in that court, and many did. Not in the local court but the international one – because they know very well that the culprits will not be brought to court in their own country.

Drakulic's S and the Muslim women who tell their stories in *I Begged Them to Kill Me* literally become the objects of consumption. They are reduced to second-class citizens whose opinions and welfare do not matter in the least.

The feeling of being reduced to second-class citizens is one that runs like a red thread through much post-1989 writing by Eastern European writers. To a male writer like Fatos Lubonja, this feeling is much more symbolic than the one mentioned above, to be sure, but it is still real. Referring to a *bonmot* concerning the role of the intellectual coined by Hungarian philosopher Gaspar Miklos Tamas, Lubonja writes:

> First, prophet – the one who develops and spreads visions for the future ...,
> Second, judge – the one who judges, over time, history, reality ...,
> Third, witness – the one who bears witness to his/her own time ...
> According to Tamas, intellectuals from the West have appropriated for themselves the twin roles of prophet and judge, and this leaves for us intellectuals from the East only the role of witness (211).[10]

10. My translation from the German.

To Dragan Velikic, there is a Europe A and a Europe B, and it will take a long time before the latter and its inhabitants will feel a part of the former. There is much work to be done by both A and B Europeans, but defining 'European literature' in such a way that it also includes the literature written by the latter is a good place to start.

Consumption may, it is hinted by some Eastern European writers, provide a short cut for B Europeans: Through consuming the same products as A Europeans, B Europeans may end up feeling – and looking like – they 'belong.' But consuming one's way to belonging may backfire in various ways. It may provide only empty satisfaction, and it may promote a development in Europe that will, culturally speaking, further the sort of popular culture that lacks in intellectual depth.

c. Copyright and European narratives:
'Copyright,' argues Kieran Dolin, 'is one of the clearest instances of the interrelation of legal and literary ideas, of literary concepts feeding into legal doctrine, and legal categories then shaping cultural practice. Not surprisingly, it is one of the focal points of Law and Literature studies.'(Dolin 62-63). Traditionally, scholars have talked about two different paradigms of copyright: A paradigm which sees copyright as the personal property of the writer and a paradigm which sees copyright as the moral right of the writer. The former is typical of Anglo-American law, whereas the latter is a poor translation of the French '*droit moral*,' a subdivision of '*droit d'auteur*,' and is characteristic of mainland European law. By contrast to Anglo-American copyright, 'authors' rights' are 'inalienable' and cannot be freely traded. Within the field of copyright, that is, we find a transatlantic dialogue of sorts going on. Some would argue that it is currently the Anglo-American copyright paradigm that is 'winning,' and that this has dire consequences for the cultural life of mainland Europe.

If the balance is tipping in favor of the Anglo-American paradigm of copyright, the way to set that balance straight again, some European copyright scholars now argue, is to look towards international human rights document such as the Universal Declaration of Human Rights, the International Covenant on Economic, Social and Cultural Rights and the European Convention on Human Rights.[11] An emphasis on human rights makes the protection of human dignity and the general common good central.

11. In the Universal Declaration it is especially Art. 27 – which talks about 'the right freely to participate in the cultural life of the community, to enjoy the arts and to share in scientific advancement and its benefits' (1) as well as 'the right to the protection of the

As I see it, copyright will become more and more important in the future. It will set the parameters for creativity by allowing or prohibiting the reproduction of vital cultural texts – texts that are constitutive of the cultural milieu in which we live.[12] Holders of copyright are in some senses able to exert monopolies over public meaning, and the more people will engage actively with commodified cultural forms – the more our culture becomes one of consumption – the more power these holders will have.

Concluding remarks

Being commissioned in 2005 to write a hymn on human rights, Italian composer Francesco Cali and Danish poet Jeppe Marsling suggested that the International Declaration of Human Rights may be compared to a tree growing on a grave. The roots of the tree will forever be tied to the grave – but the tree has found a way to grow all the same. 'Finding inspiration for an art work on justice,' wrote Marsling, who was responsible for the lyrics of the hymn,

> is not easy. It is not possible to search one's heart for the glory of human rights without having to feel the dark inhuman background out of which the declaration emerged 60 years ago. The declaration is a tree on a grave. And therefore: the most beautiful of trees. Its bitter-sweet fruits are to be handled with care.

The 'Human Rights Hymn,' which consists of four parts and a chorus, opens with a reminder of the war and the 'loss of humanity.' It then goes on to celebrate peace as 'both an end and a new beginning' and ends on the suggestion that 'out of remembrance and darkness the inspiration now surfaces and unfolds into a celebration of how we – the human race(s) – can avoid injustice' now and in the future (Marsling).

---

moral and material interests resulting from any scientific, literary or artistic production of which he is the author' (2) – that is of interest. As for the International Covenant on Economic, Social and Cultural Rights, we find in Art. 15 an almost verbatim adoption of Art. 27 of the Universal Declaration. Finally, Art. 10 of the European Convention promises everyone the right to freedom of expression, to hold opinions and to receive and impart information and ideas.

12. See Rosemary J. Coombe, *The Cultural Life of Intellectual Properties: Authorship, Appropriation, and the Law.*

The very naiveté of the lyrics of the hymn and its creator's way of talking about it are embarrassing yet at the same time endearing. And this takes me to a point made by the Danish writer Jens Christian Grøndahl in the anthology *Wrting Europe: What is European about the literatures of Europe?*, put together by Ursula Keller and Ilma Rakusa in 2003. Grøndahl points to that major European paradox: Much as European history is full of cruelty and lack of respect for human dignity, it is also characterized by the idea that each human being is special and that we are all equal. And then he continues:

> Since democracy has been instituted all over the continent, it is no longer the remote dream that is was fifty or even ten years ago; only, now all talk of universalism and European individualism may sound somewhat arrogant, even naïve – except when we talk about literature (Grøndahl 136).[13]

From the troubadours of the Middle Ages to the dissident-writers in Eastern Europe – for all of them, literature and literary endeavor has been about finding and expressing an autonomous voice that would forever object to tyrannical attempts of imposing particular norms and values on other people:

> Much like the idea of having a private life and of having a right not to have one's personal sphere violated, the novel is a European invention, and we need not be afraid of being called Eurocentric on that score ... If the history of democracy is also the history of the individual, and if it shows how the idea of individuality has grown out of the warm, secure, but also highly suffocating embrace of cultural identity, then the novel presents the possibility of telling this history (Grøndahl 137).[14]

What Grøndahl is getting at here is central to my argument. After post-modernity and post-colonialism, putting into words, discussing and updating the values that derive, to a large extent, from the European Enlightenment, is tricky business. What looks naïve and embarrassing in a political science treatise may, however, look much more palatable in a piece of literature, a piece of art or a movie. Among the most self-reflexive of art forms, literature, art and movies can do what other media cannot do. For the discussion of what Europe is, can and perhaps also ought to be, Europeans need not only their

13. My translation from the German.
14. My translation from the German.

politicians and intellectuals, but also their writers and artists. This is true in the well-known sense that literary and artistic narratives can create empathy, make their readers feel and thereby come to a better understanding of that which is important for others. But it is true in another sense, too. These narratives turn 'Project Europe' into an open project – a project which makes accessible to everyone the still unresolved tensions between local, regional, national and European identities. The future of Europe depends on the way in which such tensions are dealt with.

In exposing and exploring in a non-essentialist way issues relating to European identity/identities lies hope. The process is a very slow and sometimes also a very painful one, and there are writers and artists who strongly doubt that it will lead anywhere. 'What is Europe then?,' asks Irish writer Colm Toíbín, for example. 'It is not a culture and not an identity. It is a word we should set about undermining further as time goes by.' Yet, when it comes to Ireland's membership of the EU, Toíbín is very positive. If not for this membership, Irish women would still earn less than Irish men, and homosexuality would be a punishable offence, he admits (Toíbín 323-29). Even for a Euro-skeptic such as Toíbín, it would thus seem, 'Europe' is associated with human rights gains and with respect for individual autonomy.

Bibliography

Beck, Ulrich and Edgar Grande. *Der kosmopolitische Blick*. Frankfurt am Main: Suhrkamp 2004

---. *Macht und Gegenmacht im globalen Zeitalter*. Frankfurt am Main: Suhrkamp 2002.

---. *Das kosmopolitische Europa. Gesellschaft und Politik in der Zweiten Moderne* (both Frankfurt am Main: Suhrkamp 2004.

Coombe, Rosemary J. *The Cultural Life of Intellectual Properties: Authorship, Appropriation, and the Law*. Durham: Duke University Press 1998.

'Contesting Europe: Feminist Critiques and Globalization' – call for papers for the 'Women in German Annual Conference (WiG),' to be held at Snowbird, Utah, October 18-21, 2007. Available at <www.womeningerman.org> March 3 2007.

Dolin, Kieran. *A critical introduction to Law and Literature*. Cambridge and New York: Cambridge University Press 2007.

Drakulic, Slavenka. 'Bosnian Women Witness,' *The Nation*, March 19 2001, March 4 2009 <http://www.thenation.com/doc/20010319/drakulic>.

Glendon, Mary Ann. *Rights Talk: The Impoverishment of Political Discourse*. New York: Free Press, 1991.

Grøndahl, Jens Christian. In Ursula Keller and Ilma Rakusa, eds. *Europa schreibt. Was ist das europäische an den Literaturen Europas?* Hamburg: edition Körber-Stiftung 2003

Keller, Ursula and Ilma Rakusa, eds. *Writing Europe: What is European about the literatures of Europe?* Budapest: Central European University Press 2004.

Lubonja, Fatos. In Ursula Keller and Ilma Rakusa, eds. *Europa schreibt. Was ist das europäische an den Literaturen Europas?* Hamburg: edition Körber-Stiftung 2003.

Marsling, Jeppe. 'On the Human Rights Hymn.' Institute for Human Rights, Copenhagen 2005.

Porsdam, Helle. *From civil to human rights: Dialogues on law and humanities in the United States and Europe*. Cheltenham, UK: Edward Elgar Publishers, 2009.

---.. 'On European Narratives of Human Rights and Their Possible Implications for Copyright.' In Fiona Macmillan ed. *New Directions in Copyright Law, Vol. VI*. Cheltenham: Edward Elgar Publishers 2007

Ruttley, Philip. 'The Long Road to Unity: The Contribution of Law to the Process of European Integration since 1945.' In Anthony Pagden ed. *The Idea of Europe: From Antiquity to the European Union*. Washington, D.C.: Woodrow Wilson Center & Cambridge University Press 2002.

'The European Union: Furthering Human Rights and Democracy Across the Globe,' European Commission, External Relations, 2007.

Tibi, Bassam. *Europa ohne Identität? Leitkultur oder Wertebeliebigkeit*. Munich: Siedler, 2004.

Toíbín, Colm. In Ursula Keller and Ilma Rakusa, eds. *Europa schreibt. Was ist das europäische an den Literaturen Europas?* Hamburg: edition Körber-Stiftung 2003.